A STRAIGHTFORWARD GUIDE TO CARING FOR A DISABLED CHILD

Fifth Edition
ABIGAIL KNIGHT

S

www.straightforwardco.co.uk

© Abigail Knight Fifth Edition 2008

British Library Cataloguing in Publication data. A catalogue record for this book is available from the British Library.

ISBN   1 84716 0 73 5
ISBN 13: 9781847160 73 7

Printed by Biddles Ltd Kings Lynn Norfolk
Cover design by Bookworks Islington

Whilst every effort has been taken to ensure the information given in the book is accurate at the time the book was printed, the author and publishers recognise that information can become out of date. The book is therefore sold on condition that no responsibility for errors or omissions is assumed. The author and publishers cannot be held liable for any loss which is a result of the use of any information contained herein.

CONTENTS

INTRODUCTION

For many parents of a disabled child, the experience is made all the more traumatic by a lack of information from professionals. Not only do some parents feel shocked, saddened and alone by the fact that their child has been diagnosed as having a disability - if a diagnosis at all is made - they can be made to feel powerless by a lack of information about their child's condition and the services, support and benefits to which they and their child are entitled.

If you are one of these parents, I hope you will find this book useful and help you to ask for the things which exist to assist and support you and your child. Because of the wide range of different conditions, this book does not give any information on specific disabilities. This information can be obtained from libraries or organisations such as MENCAP or Contact a Family (see section on useful addresses). 'Caring for a Disabled Child', whilst aimed primarily at parents, may also be of interest to those who work with families of disabled children, whether this is in the health, education or social services. This book, therefore, may also be of use to staff working in such agencies. It may also be of use to students of health and social care courses, nursing, nursery nursing and social work.

A word about terms used in this book. There has been much debate about whether it is correct to say 'child with a disability' as this, many argue, emphasises the fact that the child is a child first and foremost and has a disability second. Others argue that children and adults are disabled by society, not because they have an impairment: if society (in the western world anyway) worked in a different way then children and adults with physical or mental impairments would not be disabled. This argument emphasises disability as a social construction and therefore says that it is important to say that these children and adults are 'disabled'. There are important messages in both of these terms so I shall be using them both throughout the book.

Finally and most importantly, many parents of disabled children, both those who have received a specific diagnosis for their child and those who have not, have told me that getting information about and access to services and benefits is a real battle. I hope very much that 'Caring for a Disabled Child' makes some of that battle a little easier for you to fight and eventually win.

1

REACTIONS AND EMOTIONS

When you have a disabled child you have to cope not only with practical issues, such as dealing with benefits and professionals, but also with your emotions and reactions to having a child with a disability and the feelings of relatives and friends. It is also important to consider the reactions and emotions of your disabled child's siblings.

One word of warning before starting to outline the varied reactions and emotions of different people: many of these feelings are negative ones. Although it is natural to feel negative about your child's disability as an initial reaction, remember that it isn't all bad. Children who are disabled - like all children - are both challenging and rewarding. They can bring enormous joy, and witnessing progress in their development, however small, can be wonderful.

Reactions and emotions of parents

Some parents are given the news that their child has a disability at birth or even before birth. Others receive a diagnosis after months or years, often suspecting that 'something' was wrong from an early age. Others never receive a diagnosis as their child has no specific condition.

Depending on the timing of discovering your child's disability and the way in which you discovered it, your feelings and reactions will vary in nature and intensity. However, most parents go through many of the same emotions that would be felt had they experienced bereavement. These emotions include: immediate grief, shock, disbelief, denial, anger, feeling alone and finally, acceptance and adjustment.

If you were told at your child's birth that s/he had a disability, your shock and grief may have been particularly intense. This is because when most parents are expecting a baby, they are expecting a 'normal' and 'perfect' baby. After 9 months, adjusting to a baby, whether or not s/he is disabled, is a major task. If you have been told that your child will have extra needs, this period of adjustment will be even greater. The way in which you were told about your child's disability would have had an important effect on your emotions when dealing with the news. Most parents prefer to be told as soon as possible, and together if there are 2 parents. Also it is always best to have the baby present as the child can sometimes feel a stranger or an object rather than a small human being, especially if a label describing a condition is going to be attached to him or her.

Being given inappropriate and out-of-date information at the time of diagnosis is also a common experience of many parents. Sometimes an over negative picture of the condition is given or, at the other extreme, false hopes are raised. Thankfully, the medical profession is becoming more aware of and sensitive to the needs of parents when a diagnosis is given. Unfortunately, however, there are still a number of parents who experience an insensitivity and lack of information when the news is broken. Remember though, that when you are given some news which is a shock and difficult to deal with, your capacity for taking in all what is said is very limited. The right timing of receiving information which is relevant and useful is essential. For some, the time for this after diagnosis comes quicker than for others. This needs to be judged carefully by the professional working with you. However, it is important that you ask more questions when you feel you are ready as you may not want to do this straightaway.

For some parents, a diagnosis is made a while after birth or a diagnosis can never be made at all. The vast majority of these parents will have concerns and worries about their child's development a long time before they are recognised by the medical profession. These parents are often dismissed and labeled as being neurotic. If you are one of these parents, it is important that you keep asking questions about your child and about the help you may be entitled to. Parents - like their children - are all different but may experience some or all of the following reactions and emotions when they discover their child has a disability. If you have experienced some of these, it may help you to know that you are not alone in having these feelings.

Shock

Shock is often expressed as a physical sensation such as feeling cold, nauseous, as if you are going to faint, or perspiring. Shock is an immediate reaction to some news and it is at this point that it may be particularly difficult to take in information which is given to you.

Disbelief

Not wanting to believe the news or realisation that your child is disabled is a very natural and common reaction. Denial is a way of protecting ourselves and we all do it to some extent. It is only unhealthy to deny such news if this reaction continues for a long while after the diagnosis and if it prevents you from pursuing all the necessary help and support for your child in order for s/he to develop to his or her potential.

Anger

Finding out that your child is disabled is not something that can be changed. Not having a choice or control over the situation can often lead to frustration and anger, which again, is a common and natural emotion to experience. Anger, in small doses, can sometimes be

10

constructive as it can be energising, but sometimes it turns in on itself and leads to depression.

Depression

Depression can express itself through feelings of pessimism and hopelessness and lead to difficulties in eating and sleeping. Crying frequently and losing interest, energy and enthusiasm in life around you are typical signs. If you think you are suffering from depression and recognise some or all of these signs, it is important to seek professional help, from your G.P., health visitor, social services or voluntary agency. The end of this chapter and the next give more details on sources of help and support. You may be offered medication to help your depression, such as anti-depressants. It is your decision whether or not to take them, but if you do, it is also important to express your feelings to a skilled listener and to seek practical and emotional help such as a parent group and services such as day care and/or respite care to give yourself some space.

Grief

Although depression is a serious reaction to the news that your child is disabled and something which needs professional help, remember that feeling a certain amount of sadness and grief is totally understandable and must be expected. These feelings are very similar to those when you have lost someone very close to you. Although you have not lost your child in terms of his or her life, you have lost the child you hoped to have and have to start changing the expectations you have for him or her.

Guilt

Many parents experience a great sense of guilt about having a disabled child. If you can identify with this, you may have blamed yourself - or your partner - for carrying a particular gene or doing something, or not doing something, during pregnancy. You may also feel like you have been punished for something. Remember that in the vast majority of cases, having a disabled child is out of our control and cannot be helped.

Along with feeling guilty, you may also feel like you have let everyone down, i.e. your partner, your family and other children. You may also feel embarrassed to face people and to go out with your child, cutting yourself from friends. Later on in this chapter, there will be more discussion about the reactions and emotions of friends and how to cope with these.

Negative Feelings Towards Your Child

One emotion that is particularly difficult to deal with and which most parents feel terribly guilty about is feeling negative about the look of their child. Many children who have disabilities of course do not look different; many do, however, and particularly at first, some parents find this hard to deal with and accept. It is important to say that it often takes a while before a bond develops between a child and his or her parent(s). Many parents say that at first their child feels like a stranger to begin with, especially is he or she needs a lot of physical care. It is often only when the young child starts to respond through smiling or making noises other than crying and appears to be more like a real person with his/her own character, that they feel really comfortable being with them.

You may also at times feel over protective towards your disabled child. Again this is a normal reaction and is probably quite instinctive. It does become problematic, however, if being over protective prevents the child developing his or her own independence to the best of his or her ability.

If you have feelings of wanting to harm your child, you must seek help immediately. Help can be obtained from your G.P., social services (emergency social services if it is outside office hours - the number will be under your local council in the telephone directory) or organisations such as Parentline, CRY-SIS and the NSPCC (details at the end of this chapter and in the section on useful addresses.

If you feel like hitting your child, it is always best to leave the room even if you have to leave the child crying. Crying will not harm the child, hitting him or her will. If you feel the need to express your frustration, anger or aggression, hit something else, like a pillow, very hard. In any event, you should always pick up the phone to someone, whether it is a friend, relative, professional or helpline, before you lash out.

How to Cope with Your Reactions and Emotions

Most of the emotions and reactions listed are very negative feelings. Remember that, with time and support, the vast majority of parents do cope. Not only do they cope but they also get great pleasure from their disabled child and find them and witnessing their development extremely rewarding.

The best way of coping with all of these feelings is to talk about them as openly as possible with friends, family, other parents and sympathetic professionals. Let yourself cry and share your anger, guilt and frustration. Supportive parent groups are run by MENCAP and Contact a Family and other organisations for specific disabilities, such as the Down's Syndrome Association. Phone the national organisation and find out about local groups. Contact a Family also runs groups for parents of children of specific, and sometimes rare, conditions. Their phone number is listed at the end of this chapter, whilst other useful organisations are listed at the end of the book.

It is also important to attempt to continue as normal a life as possible. Going out to see friends, for example, and doing the things you enjoy doing are important ways of preventing the needs of your disabled child, whilst being of primary importance, becoming the only focus for you and your family. Clearly, seeing friends and doing things you enjoy are often easier said than done, especially if you have little practical support and/or you have sole responsibility for

13

the care of your child. Seeking help from statutory (e.g. health or social services) or voluntary agencies may enable you to find the practical and emotional assistance you need.

Finally, it is worth noting that although you may stop feeling saddened and guilty about your child, some of these feelings may return just as you though you were coping well. These feelings will pass as they did before, probably making you feel stronger than ever.

Reactions and emotions of partners

If you have a partner, s/he is likely to experience many of the reactions and emotions already described, but it is not likely to respond in exactly the same way as you. Remember that s/he is a different and unique person!

Whatever you and your partner is feeling, it is always best to try and discuss and share each other's feelings. It may sometimes be hard to understand why your partner feels something if you do not, but it is important to listen to and respect these feelings. Bottling up emotions often results in increased tensions and misunderstandings so talking is vital.

Remember you won't agree on everything to do with your child's disability and how to bring him or her up, something you have most likely discovered in your relationship about other issues. It will sometimes be necessary for you to compromise, therefore, and to try and see your partner's point of view.

It is probably true to say that the relationship between parents is one of the most significant factors in how a family adjusts to a disability and how the disabled child, him or herself, copes. Having a disabled child undoubtedly puts a strain on a relationship but this is not to say that the relationship will fail. The most successful partnerships seem to be where each person is prepared to share his or her feelings, supports the other through difficult times and puts great value on spending quality time together.

If it is not possible for you and your partner to discuss and respect each other's feelings and the tensions and conflicts become too much, it is always best to request help from a skilled professional, such as a counsellor (from Relate, for example) rather than let the issues to go on unresolved. However much you may try and cover up the difficulties in your relationship, children - including disabled children of course - are sensitive to and pick up vibes, and will be affected by them.

If your partner is male and he is your child's father, it may be that he will experience the disability, particularly at first, in a more negative way. Generally speaking, mothers bond more quickly with children and the father may, to begin with, experience feelings of rejection towards the child. Involving him as much as possible in the child's care, appointments with professionals and in the child's general development may help change this initial reaction. In time, and with this involvement, he will most likely become a source of strength, sharing with you the anxieties, challenges and happiness in caring for your child.

Reactions and emotions of relatives

Your relatives need to be told very soon that your child is disabled, if a diagnosis is made. It is always best to tell people with your child present, especially if s/he is a baby. Your relatives will also experience many of the emotions and reactions already described in this chapter. Close relatives such as the child's grandparents are likely to feel a sense of guilt and worry that they have been responsible if there is a genetic problem. It is also possible that they will have old fashioned views about disability and may need up-to-date information and the child's condition and what it may mean, in a practical sense, to care for the child.

Relatives may want to help by babysitting and doing housework, for example, and this may assist them in coping with their feelings and possible guilt.

Reactions and emotions of friends

If you receive a diagnosis when your child is a baby, try and tell your friends about your child's disability as soon as possible. Many parents put this off and it then becomes more and more difficult, sometimes resulting in them avoiding going out with the baby in case someone sees him or her and notices that 'something is wrong'.

You will probably feel relieved once you have told friends about your child's disability. Sometimes, though, friends will feel uncomfortable when you tell them and will not know how to respond. This is because many people are afraid of disability and don't know how to deal with it. Again, if they can see the child/baby as soon as possible, this will reinforce the fact that the child is a child first and foremost, and will make them concentrate less on the disability or condition.

Like relatives, they will often feel better if they can help you out and feel as if they are doing something constructive. So if they are willing to help you, ask them to do something practical and specific, like a bit of shopping or babysitting, which will make them feel more relaxed and able to offer practical support.

Reactions and emotions of your child's siblings

It is important to tell your other child(ren) about your disabled child as soon as possible. Otherwise, they will pick up vibes from you and the rest of your family, is likely to overhear conversations and worry that something is wrong. Many children fantasize about situations they have sensed and start to believe they are to blame. They, therefore, need both information and reassurance early on.

How much you tell your child(ren), though, clearly depends on how old they are. Children under the age of 3 are still too young to understand details about their sibling's disability or condition. But they can be told you are feeling sad and that his or her sibling needs lots of care and attention.

16

Children this age may present more difficult behaviour in response to this. They may have more tantrums or cling to you or show attention seeking behaviour.

Older children can be told a bit more about their sibling's disability. Use simple terms and do not describe the disability as an illness as this will confuse them. Most children will understand the concept of disability or handicap or the explanation that your disabled child cannot do as much as other children.

Much older siblings like teenagers are likely to respond in much the same way as adults and experience some of the emotions described earlier in this chapter. You need to give them time and space to express these feelings.

Although brothers and sisters will be very significant people in your disabled child's life, it is important to remember two main principles:

i) share your time between all your children. Siblings should have special time with their parents, even if this means organising respite care (e.g. babysitting or time being cared by others in a family or residential setting) for your disabled child;

ii) siblings need to be reassured that it is not their responsibility to take on the care of their disabled sibling when you are no longer around.

Sometimes siblings are teased about their disabled brother or sister, perhaps by other children at school. They are likely to feel upset and angry about this. It is important to be aware of and sensitive to this possibility and to listen to their feelings.

Siblings can be helped in coping with their feelings about having a disabled brother or sister through siblings groups which are sometimes run by voluntary agencies or social services departments, or by involving the class teacher, who may be able to help by

17

initiating a discussion about disability in class, or through children's books on disability.

Like partners, relatives and friends, try and enable your other children to become involved in your disabled child's life and development. You will probably find that although some difficulties may exist, such as jealousy and resentment, overall, siblings will become caring and supportive friends to their disabled brother or sister.

Now read the key points from Chapter 1 overleaf.

KEY POINTS

- You will experience a number of emotions when you discover your child has a disability, such as shock, grief, denial, anger, guilt, and possibly depression and negative feelings towards your child

- You may not experience all of these emotions and some of them may come and go

- Your partner, relatives, friends and older children may also experience some of these feelings but they won't react in exactly the same way as you - they are different people - so try and respect their feelings

- Try and involve your partner, relatives, friends and older children in your disabled child's care and development

- Remember that however bad you feel, you are not alone, as there are others in the same or similar situation. Also it is worth bearing in mind that the vast majority of parents do cope and end up enjoying caring for their disabled child. Meeting other parents through organisations may be very helpful to you

USEFUL ORGANISATIONS

Contact A Family
209-211 City Road, London EC1V 1JN
020 7608 8700
Helpline: 0808 808 3555   Open Monday to Friday 10 am-4 pm and
Monday 5.30pm-7.30pm.
Email: info@cafamily.org.uk
Website: www.cafamily.org.uk

Contact a family also helps families with children affected by similar
impairments and conditions get in touch with each other. Visit the
website www.makingcontact.org.uk.
Information and support groups for specific (including rare) conditions.

MENCAP
123 Golden Lane, London EC1Y ORT
020 7454 0454
Information and local groups.
Website: www.mencap.org.uk

Learning Disability Helpline: 0808 808 1111 Open 10-4 Monday to
Friday.
*One Stop Shop information and advice on a range of issues, including support,
welfare benefits, health, housing, education and
employment.*

PARENTLINE PLUS
530 Highgate Studios, 53-79 Highgate Road, London NW5 1TL.
Helpline: 0808 800 2222
Website: www.parentlineplus.org.uk
Support for parents and children.

CRY-SIS
BM Cry-sis, London WC1 3XX
Helpline: 084501 228669-9am-10pm 7 days a week
info@cry-sis.org.uk
www.crysis.org.uk
Helpline a*nd support for parents of crying children.*

NSPCC (National Society for the Prevention of Cruelty to Children)
42 Curtain Road, London EC2A 3NH
020 7825 2500
Website: www.nspcc.org.uk
Helpline for adults: 0800 800 500
Childline: 0800 1111

RELATE (RELATIONSHIP GUIDANCE)
Herbert Gray College, Little Church Street, Rugby CV21 3AP
0845 456 1310
website: www.relate.org.uk
Runs counselling for couples throughout the country.

CARERS UK
20-25 Glasshouse Yard
London EC1A 4JT
020 7490 8818
Carers Line: 0808 808 7777 (Monday-Friday 10-12 and 2-4)
Website: www.carersuk.org.uk
Provides an information and advice service to anyone with a caring role.

For more useful organizations, please see the last section of this book.

2

WHO CAN HELP? WHO DOES WHAT?

When you have a disabled child, you will come into contact with a variety of professionals from health services, social services, education and voluntary agencies, throughout your son or daughter's childhood and early adulthood. This can sometimes feel overwhelming especially if you feel confused about each professional's role, how they can help you and your child, and who employs them. This chapter, therefore, attempts to define clearly and simply the different professionals' roles and how they can help.

You may hear the terms, statutory and voluntary agencies. Statutory services are the ones run by the state under legislation, such as the health service (e.g. NHS and Community Care Act 1990), social services (e.g. The Children Act 1989), education (e.g. the special Educational Needs and Disability Act 2001), housing and so on.

Increasingly you will come across the term 'children's services' instead of social services and education departments. This is because under the government Green Paper, *Every child Matters* (2003) and the subsequent Children Act 2004, there is a duty on local authorities to integrate their services for children and families into children's services rather than to continue separating them into social services and education. Education, social care and health services for children are also being integrated under children's trusts and children's centers.

Health services are run by trusts and regional health authorities which usually cover different areas from the other services mentioned, which are run by your local council. Voluntary agencies in contrast are run by committees made up of interested volunteers and often employ paid staff to run services, such as play schemes, residential care and so on. They are also pressure groups as they normally work for a particular group in society and contribute to a campaign which aims to improve the quality of life for those people. MENCAP is a good example of a voluntary agency. Its policies are ultimately governed by a voluntary committee, but it employs numerous paid staff in its national headquarters and in many local organisations throughout the country. It runs services for children and adults with a learning disability and their families and also campaigns for better rights for those people.

Having a disabled child means coming into contact with professionals from the health service from an early stage. Below is a list of the professionals you may encounter and what they do.

HEALTH SERVICE

Health Visitor

Health Visitors are nurses who have had a year's additional training to specialise in working in the community with a broader public health/health promotion role. They officially work with all client groups and ages, although in practice the vast majority of their time is spent working with families of children aged 0 to 5. Most of their role involves advising parents on issues such as feeding, growth and development and immunisations.

Specialist Health Visitor

Not all health authorities employ specialist health visitors. Where they do, they have a particular interest, or specialist training, in both physically and learning disabled children. Apart from the role described above, the specialist health visitor should also be able to offer practical advice on caring for a disabled child and to liaise with other health staff and other agencies to help you obtain all available services. They should also be able to offer you counselling or advice on where you can receive counselling.

G.P (General Practitioner)

The G.P.'s role is to provide health care for your disabled child and your family, either by dealing with any issue him or herself or by referring you to more specialist services. For example, the G.P. may refer your disabled child to specialist services such as a psychologist, physiotherapist, occupational therapist, speech therapist or a consultant paediatrician (see below for definitions).

Consultant Paediatrician

The Consultant Paediatrician is the most senior of a team of doctors specialising in working with children.

Clinical Medical Officer (CMO)

The Clinical Medical Officer is a doctor who is present at child health clinics and who carries out school medicals.

Hospital Doctors and Nurses

A number of titles are used to describe doctors who work in a hospital and distinguish between senior and junior doctors. The following list starts with the most senior and works down:

Consultant
Senior Registrar - Sen. Reg.
Registrar - Reg.
Senior House Officer - SHO
House Officer - HO
Student Doctor or Medical Student

There are also many different types of nurses. Some of the main ones are listed below:

Ward Sister: responsible for the day to day running of a ward and all the nurses working there.
Charge Nurse: the male equivalent of the ward sister.
Registered General Nurse - RGN
Registered Sick Children's Nurse - RSCN
Registered Mental Nurse - RMN
Registered Nurse Mental Handicap - RNMH
Staff Nurse - SN: has completed a period if training in nursing.
Enrolled Nurse - EN: a nurse who has completed a shorter period of training than a staff nurse.
Clinical Nurse Specialist - CNS: works within a specialist area.
Senior Nurse: is in charge of the management of a ward or department. Is sometimes known as the Clinical Nurse Manager or Ward Manager.

You may hear the terms, locum or agency. These terms refer to a temporary member of staff who covers for sickness and/or holidays.

Physiotherapist

A physiotherapist, or physio. for short, helps the child's or adult's bodily co-ordination, muscle tone and motor control, such as learning to walk and sitting up straight, by using a variety of methods such as exercises and massage. The ultimate purpose of physiotherapy is to help the child or adult gain as much independence as possible.

Occupational Therapist (O.T.)

O.T.s are trained to look at self-help and appropriate equipment for children and/or adults, which help them be as independent as

25

possible. They may teach children with disabilities individual skills such as washing, dressing, feeding and toileting and may be able to help with behaviour problems. A large part of their role is assessing disabled children and adults for adaptations in the home (e.g. a special chair, bath seat) and monitoring them after they have been installed, to ensure the child or adult can live as independently as possible.

Occupational Therapists can be employed by the health service, social services departments and by the housing department.

Clinical Psychologist

Clinical Psychologists are specialists in assessing and treating children and adults with behaviour and/or emotional difficulties. Working with learning disabled children will be part of their training and they will be able to help the child develop effective and adaptive skills in areas such as communication, coping, problem solving and relationships. The Clinical Psychologist will do this by talking at length to the family and other professionals about the problem behaviour and by observing the child/young adult and will then devise a programme or set of guidelines for the family and other professionals (e.g. school staff) to follow when they are with the child.

Incontinence Advisors

Most health authorities have a Continence Advisor. Ask your G.P., Paediatrician or health visitor.

Speech and Language Therapist

Speech and language therapists assess and treat children and adults who have speech, language and hearing difficulties. They help to correct any speech disorders and will advise parents and other professionals, especially school staff, on how they can help the child to improve his or her speech. Unfortunately, most areas have a severe shortage of speech therapists.

Audiologist

An audiologist works with children who have hearing difficulties and will also be able to advise on aids to improve hearing.

Access to any of the above professionals described is usually through your G.P. or other health professional, such as Paediatrician or health visitor.

As your child gets older, you may find services offered by your local social services department very helpful. Some of what they do is listed below:

SOCIAL SERVICES/CHILDREN'S SERVICES

Social Worker

Social workers assess children or adults and their carers/families, who may need help and support of local services (e.g. respite care), in order to promote their welfare. Social workers have a statutory duty to become involved with a family where it is .thought that a child is at risk of harm. They may also be able to offer advice on benefits and be involved in the statementing process (see chapter on education) by writing a social report. Increasingly social services or children's services departments have specialist teams of social workers who work only with disabled children and their families.

Occupational Therapist (O.T.)

The role of the O.T. has been described under the health service section. The O.T can also be employed by the children's services department. They will either work as part of a team working with both adults or children or they may work as part of a multi-disciplinary social work team for disabled children and their families.

Care Manager

Care managers work with adults who have complex needs (e.g. an adult with a physical or learning disability, mental health problems or the elderly) and is responsible for the co-ordination of services for an individual. Care managers can come from a social work, nursing, occupational therapy or physiotherapy background. Some work for Community Learning Disability or Mental Handicap teams who work with learning disabled adults. They normally start being involved with a young person who has a learning disability around the time of their 16th or 17th birthday, so that the transfer from child care services can be as smooth as possible. Care Managers may be involved in obtaining respite care or long term care away from the family home for learning disabled adults.

Childcare: day nurseries, children's centers, playgroups, childminding and out-of school provision

Under the Children Act 1989, disabled children are automatically considered to be 'in need' and are therefore entitled to some day care. This entitlement has been strengthened by the recent Children Act 2006, which places a duty on local authorities to provide childcare for disabled children. There are many forms of childcare and these include private day nurseries, children's centers, pre-school and playgroups, childminders and out of school provision, run by the local authority or voluntary and private organizations. The important characteristic to check out is that they are registered and monitored by ofsted. Not only does this ensure that certain standards have been reached but also means that fees may be claimed back through child care tax credits.

Contact your local children's services or children's information services for advice about what is available and how it may be funded. Advice and information may also be obtained from the Childcare

28

Link Freephone Services on 08000 96 02 96 or www.childcarelink.org.uk.

Short-term breaks or respite care

Most children's services run some sort of respite care services for disabled children and their families. This will either be a family based service, where your child will stay with another family, who has been thoroughly assessed and approved, for short-breaks (e.g. overnight, weekends occasionally) or will be a residential home. Respite care is usually difficult to obtain as there is so much demand for this type of service, so it is important to ask about this quite early on and be prepared to wait a while.

Register of children with disabilities

Under the Children Act 1989, social services departments have a duty to set up a register of disabled children in their local area. This is so they can plan for future services for children who have disabilities.

Help with transport

Social services departments administer the travel permit for disabled people (including children) and the blue badge scheme for disabled drivers or the carers of disabled children/adults who drive them around on a regular basis. More details about this can be found in chapter 6.

For most of the above services you will not need an allocated social worker as not every family of a disabled child will be able to have one. Your first port of call to gain access to any of these services is, therefore, through a duty social worker who will work in your local social services office. Look up the address and telephone number in your telephone directory. It is always best to ring and find out the time the duty social worker is available and/or to make an appointment

By the time your child is 4 or 5, you will have more contact with the education services than with any other service. There is more information on education in chapter 4.

Early support

The Early Support Programme is a government initiative in England which has the aim of improving services for disabled children under age 5 and their families. For more information about this programme, visit the Early Support website: www.earlysupport.org.uk

EDUCATION

Special Needs Education Department

Most Education Departments of local councils will have a specific special needs education section. You should be able to find this under your local council in the telephone directory. This section will deal with the statementing of children who have special needs or disabilities (a statement is a document that sets out a child's special educational needs and extra help that she or he should get. See chapter 4 for more details on statementing) and will have a list of all the special schools in your area.

Special Educational Needs Co-ordinator (SENCO)

This is a member of staff of a school or early education setting who has the responsibility for co-ordinating the special needs provision within the school. This person is usually a teacher but in a small school, this responsibility may be taken on by the head teacher or deputy head.

Education Psychologist

An education psychologist is a specialist in how children and young people develop and learn. They work closely with teachers and parents as well as the child, to assess and treat a child who may be experiencing difficulties in their learning and/or in their social and emotional well-being at school.

Portage

Portage is a pre-school teaching service which helps parents to teach their baby/child whose development is delayed. Portage Services normally involve a home visitor coming to the home about once a week, deciding with the parents or carer what the baby or child needs to learn and how this should be attained. In some areas Portage is available through social services or health.

Peripatetic teacher

This is a teacher who works in several schools.

You will not necessarily have any contact with voluntary agencies but many parents find the services, information and support that they gain from them invaluable.

VOLUNTARY SECTOR

As discussed at the beginning of this chapter, voluntary agencies are set up to work for specific groups in society, such as Age Concern for the elderly or MIND for those with mental health problems. There are many voluntary organisations for disabled children, some of which are big national agencies with local branches (e.g. MENCAP, ASBAH), and some of which are smaller and are only locally based. Some of these voluntary organisations work for all disabled children (e.g. MENCAP) whilst some are set up for children with a specific disability (e.g. Down's Syndrome Association, National Autistic Society). Contact a Family is a good organisation to contact for unusual or non-specific disabilities.

Most voluntary agencies offer a variety of services, which include the following:

- contact with other parents through support groups;

- telephone or drop-in advice service;

- playschemes, toy libraries, playgroups or baby sitting;

- family-based respite care;

- a regular newsletter;

- information about specific disabilities or conditions;

- information about local services for disabled children and welfare
  benefits and
- general support and advocacy when liaising with benefit agencies and other authorities, such as education, social services, health and housing.

A list of all the main voluntary organisations for disabled children can be found at the end of this book.

Now read the key points from Chapter 2 overleaf.

KEY POINTS

- Help with caring for your disabled child is available from professionals working in children's services, children's trusts and children's centers. These integrate services provided by health, social services and education departments. Help is also available from a variety of voluntary organizations, either nationally or locally.

- Most health professionals can be accessed through your G.P. or health visitor so ask them if you and your child can be referred to specialist services;

- Most services offered by children's services, such as respite care, day care and help with equipment and transport can be obtained, in the first instance, through a duty social worker. You can find the number of your local social services office in the telephone directory. Phone first and find out the opening times and/or to make an appointment. Find out if your local social services department has a specialist team for children with disabilities;

- Your disabled child may need to attend a special school or s/he may be able to go to a mainstream school, where extra help may be available. Your child's statement of special education needs will make recommendations. See chapter 4 for more information;

- Voluntary organisations are a good source of information and support. Many organisations have local branches. Use the list at the end of this book or ask your G.P., health visitor or local social services office.

3

FINANCES

Many parents feel guilty or stigmatised about claiming money to look after their child. Remember that benefits are not a privilege or a handout; they are a right and are designed to meet the extra costs incurred when caring for a child with a disability, such as extra clothing, heating and transport. It is therefore very important that you claim every thing you and your child is entitled to.

This chapter outlines the welfare benefits you and your family may be entitled to if you have a disabled child. It also gives information about another source of help - the Family Fund - if your child is severely disabled, and advice about leaving money in a will to a learning disabled son or daughter, a worry of many parents.

WELFARE BENEFITS
Income Support
Income Support is a means-tested benefit to help people who are unemployed and do not qualify for unemployment benefit because they have not paid enough national insurance contributions or work less than 16 hours a week and do not have enough money to live on. You will not qualify for Income Support if you have savings of more than £16,000, or £12,000 if over 60. There are different rates of income support depending on your age: for example, the rate in 2008/9 for those age 18-24 is £47.95 per week; for those aged 25 or over, the rate is £60.50 for a single person.

On top of the basic rate of income support, premiums may be added for people with additional needs, such as people with children. They are as follows:

Family Premium - if you have at least one child.

Disabled Child Premium - if you have a child who is getting Disabled Living Allowance for care or mobility at any rate, (see below) or who is registered blind. This premium is not always given automatically, so make sure you claim it if you qualify..

Lone Parent Premium - if you are bringing up children on your own.

Carer Premium - if your child receives Disability Living Allowance or if you receive Invalid Care Allowance.

There are other premiums for long-term sick or disabled people and for people aged 60 or over.

If you get Income Support, you or anyone you claim for will also get: free prescriptions, free eyesight tests and vouchers to help with the cost of glasses, free school meals, free NHS dental treatment, help with the cost of travelling to hospital for NHS treatment, free milk and vitamins for pregnant women and for children up to 5 years old, and cold weather payments if your benefit includes Disabled Child Premium, or if you have a child under 5.

If you want more information about Income Support call Freeline Social Security on 0800 666555, or get in touch with your local Social Security Office (used to be called Benefits Agency).

Disability Living Allowance (DLA)
This benefit is not means-tested, i.e. it is paid to people according to their needs and not their earnings.

Disability Living Allowance is payable in 2 parts: care component and mobility component. Either or both components can be claimed. The care component is paid at three different rates and the mobility component at two. The higher rate of the mobility component can now be paid from the age of 3 years whilst the lower rate can only be claimed from 5 years. The care component has a lower limit of 3 months. DLA only applies to children and adults under the age of 66. After that, Attendance Allowance applies.

35

Care Component

If, because of a physical or mental disability, your child needs a lot of looking after or help with personal care, s/he should be entitled to the care component. To qualify, a child must have needed extra help for three months and must be likely to need extra help for a further six months or more. You can claim before the three months are up if you think your child will qualify.

Children or adults not expected to live longer than six months do not have to wait for three months and should be paid the higher rate of the care component immediately, regardless of the amount of care needed.

Sometimes keeping a diary showing the extra help your child needs can mean the difference between getting DLA or not or between getting different rates. A diary may be helpful if your child's need for attention is unpredictable, or changes from day to day; your child's condition is getting worse; you need to show, for example, times you have had to get up to look after your child in the night and why, and the times you are able to get back to bed; or you want to show your child's need for continual supervision to prevent substantial danger to him or herself or others.

The care component rates for 2008/2009 are:

higher rate	£67 per week.
middle rate	£44.85 per week.
lower rate	£17.75 per week.

Mobility Component

If a person needs help getting around, s/he may qualify for the mobility component of DLA. The higher rate of the mobility component is paid to people with severe walking difficulties from age 3 years. The lower mobility rate is aimed at children or adults who can walk but need supervision when out of doors. This can only be claimed from age 5. People who cannot walk at all, who have severe difficulties in walking or who are deaf and blind should qualify for the higher rate. People who have severe behavioural problems should also qualify for the higher rate, provided that they also get the higher rate of the care component.

Those who do not qualify for the higher mobility rate may be able to get the lower rate if they can walk but need guidance or supervision from someone else when outdoors.

The rates for the mobility component of DLA in 2008-2009 are:

higher   £46.75 per week.
lower   £17.75 per week.

Claiming DLA

You can obtain a DLA claim pack from your local Social Security Office or by telephoning the Benefit Enquiry Line on Freephone 0800 882200 or 0800 243355 (minicom) or 0800 220674 in Northern Ireland.

The claim pack is very lengthy and complicated. You are more likely to be successful in your claim if you can find someone to help you with the form. You could ask your health visitor, a social worker (particularly if your social services department has a social work team for children with disabilities), adviser at a local voluntary agency or Citizens Advice Bureau.

If you are not happy with the outcome of your application for DLA, you can ask for a review within three months of the date the decision was sent to you. You can ask for a review at any time if your child's condition changes and you think s/he may be eligible for a different rate of DLA, or if the original decision ignored or misunderstood some relevant fact of your child's case. If you are still not happy after the review, you have the right to appeal to an Independent Disability Appeal Tribunal within three months of the date you received the review decision. If you are appealing, it is advisable to seek expert advice from a Citizens Advice Bureau.

Invalid Carer's Allowance (from April 2007).

This is a weekly cash allowance for anyone of any age (from October 28th 2002) who spends at least 35 hours a week looking after someone who gets the higher or middle rate of DLA for personal care. To qualify, you do not have to be related to the person you care for nor live at the same address.

ICA is a taxable allowance but you can still earn up to £84 per week, after deductions, while you are claiming ICA. You cannot get ICA if you are receiving a national insurance benefit such as Widow's Pension or Invalidity Benefit. If you receive Income Support and ICA, the amount of the ICA will be taken off your Income Support. It is still worth claiming both benefits, however, because you will be entitled to the Carer Premium worth £26.35 per week. Make sure you claim the Carer Premium if you qualify for DLA and Income support as it is not always given automatically.

You can get a claim form for ICA from your local Social Security Office (previously Benefits Agency) or Post Office or by telephoning the Benefit Enquiry Line free on 0800 882200 or 0800 243355 (minicom) or 0800 220674 in Northern Ireland.

If you want more information about income support and other benefits, call the benefits Enquiry Line on 0800 88 22 00 (0800 22 06 74 in Northern Ireland).

Working Tax Credit and child's tax credit (WTC)

These are means tested benefits for individuals and families working more than 16 hours per week. The amount you will receive depends on how much you earn and for the child tax credit, how many children you have, whether they are disabled and how much you spend on childcare. The income threshold is quite high (about £55,000) so it is worth applying. These tax credits are administered by the Inland Revenue. Phone their helpline on 0845 300 3900 or look on www.inlandrevenue.gov.uk/tax credits.

Social Fund

If you are on Income Support and you or someone in you family is disabled or seriously ill you may be able to get a Community Care Grant to pay for certain items which you cannot afford out of your weekly benefit. These may include clothing, bedding, laundry, equipment, minor structural repairs, gas and electricity reconnection charges, redecoration and furnishings, heaters, safety items and fares to visit a close relative in hospital. Any savings over £500 will be deducted from the grant (£1000 if you are aged 60 years or over).

It is up to the Social Security Office whether you get a grant or not. If you apply for a grant you may be turned down or offered a budgeting loan instead. If you accept a loan you will have to pay it back out of your weekly benefit.

For more details ask for Social Security Office for form SF300.

Fares to Hospital

If you are on Income Support or Working Families Tax Credit you are entitled to travel costs to and from hospital for NHS treatment when escorting your child. If you are not getting these benefits but are on a low income, you may still be able to get help.

To find out more, ask for leaflet H1 'NHS Hospital Travel Costs' at the hospital or from your local Benefits Agency.

Road Tax Exemption (Vehicle Excise Duty)

If your child gets the higher rate of the mobility component of DLA, you should have been sent a Vehicle Excise Duty exemption form by the DSS automatically.

If you have not received a form, write to the Disability Allowance Unit, Warbreck House, Warbreck Hill, Blackpool, FT2 OTE.

You will not be able to claim exemption from road tax if your child receives only the lower rate of the mobility component of DLA. Contact DVLA on 0870 240 0010.

Housing Benefit

This is a benefit to help you pay your rent or service charges if you are on Income Support or a low income and have less than £16,000 savings. Savings over £6,000 affect rates of benefit on a sliding scale. No help is available towards charges paid to close relatives such as parents. The arrangements must be commercial, for example, with a landlord, housing association or local council.

You need to go to your local council Housing Department for information about claiming Housing Benefit.

Council Tax Benefit

This is financial help from a local council towards your Council Tax bill. If you are on Income Support or a low income you may be able to claim help up to 100% of your bill.

People who are severely mentally disabled may not have to pay Council Tax. Disability reductions are also available if you or a child have a major disability and therefore require a second bathroom, kitchen or other space to meet your needs.

Contact your local council or your local Citizens Advice Bureau for a list of exemptions and reductions and how to apply

Benefits After Age 16.

These include Income Support, Incapacity Benefit, and Disability Living Allowance. These will be covered in chapter 7.

THE FAMILY FUND

The Family Fund Trust is an independent organization registered as a charity and financed by the Department of Health. The fund's purpose is to ease the stress on families who care for severely disabled children under 16, by providing grants and information related to the care of the child.

The Trust helps families who are living in the United Kingdom and caring at home for a severely disabled child under 16 and whose income before deductions is not more than £23,000 per year (correct in 2007 and reviewed annually) and who have savings of £18,000 or less. The Trust cannot help children in the care of the local authority.

The fund can give lump sums for specific items that arise from the care of the child, such as extra bedding, clothing, a washing machine, tumble dryer, holidays, outings, driving lessons, and play equipment. After applying, you will be visited by one of the Family Fund's visitors who will make an assessment.

If you do receive financial help from the Family Fund, you can apply again when a new need arises, as long as your child and family still meet the Family Fund criteria. However, the fund is unlikely to help again within 12 months of having made a grant unless there is a particularly urgent need.

To apply, write giving the full name and date of birth of your child and brief details of his/her disability, the types of help you need and whether you have been in touch with the fund before, to:

> The Family Fund
> Unit 4 Alpha Court
> Monks Cross Drive
> Huntington
> York Y32 9WN
> 0845 130 4542
> info@familyfund.org.uk
> www.familyfund.org.uk

The Family Fund also produces some very useful information sheets on adaptations to housing, bedding, benefits checklist, deafness/communication, equipment for daily living, holidays, hyperactivity, transport and a guide to the opportunities available to young disabled people called 'After 16 – what's new?'. For other useful publications produced by the Family Fund Trust, please see the section on useful reading at the end of this book.

LEAVING MONEY IN A WILL TO YOUR LEARNING DISABLED SON OR DAUGHTER.

If money is left by will directly to an adult who is not able to deal with it or issue a valid receipt for it because s/he is mentally or learning disabled, a complicated situation may arise where the Court of Protection has to become involved. A receiver appointed by the Court of Protection has power to receive money or property and to deal with it on behalf of someone who is 'mentally disordered' within the meaning of the Mental Health Act 1983 and is unable to manage his/her affairs. Because a receiver would be appointed after your death, you will not have any say over who this person may be or how the property or money left to your son or daughter may be used.

Instead, when it is possible or certain that an adult with learning disabilities will be unable to handle money left to him or her, you should consider setting up a trust for him/her, which will become operational on your death and will last for your son or daughter's lifetime. Trustees, who could be a friend or relative, are appointed to hold the property and/or money and pay it or deal with it on your son or daughter's behalf as you would like.

One great problem, however, in leaving money to a learning disabled son or daughter who is dependent on state benefits, is that once the capital goes beyond £8,000 they will lose their benefit. It is possible to get round this with the help of a solicitor, by setting up a carefully worded trust. Small irregular payments can be paid without affecting Income Support, and can be used as the trustee decides. It could be used for things like holidays or equipment such as a television.

Where children under eighteen are concerned, solicitors will usually recommend that money is left upon a specific form of trust, whether or not the children have learning disabilities, as the law limits a minor's ability to give a valid receipt and to deal with money or property.

For more information, MENCAP have produced a guide to leaving money to people with a learning disability, called 'Leaving money by Will' (free of charge). You should also see a Solicitor for more information and advice. MENCAP's legal department can sometimes offer advice to solicitors on this issue.

Now read the key points from chapter three overleaf.

KEY POINTS

- If you are caring for a disabled child you may be eligible for cash benefits. Make sure you are claiming all you're entitled to by going through this list:

- Disability Living Allowance (DLA)
- Invalid Care Allowance (ICA)/ Carer's Allowance
- Road Tax Exemption
- Fares to hospital
- Working Families Tax Credit
- Income Support
- Social Fund
- Housing Benefit
- Council Tax Benefit
- Further benefits at age 16:   Income Support

                                            Incapacity Benefit

- Disabled Persons Tax Credit.

  - The Family Fund is a good source of financial help for specific items to do with the care of your child, if s/he is under age 16 and has a severe physical and/or learning disability.

  - If you want to leave money or property to your son or daughter who is learning disabled when s/he is over 18 years old, it is best to set up a trust for him or her and appoint a trustee rather than the Court of Protection becoming involved.

USEFUL ORGANISATIONS

Your local Citizens Advice Bureau will be able to help you with benefits and filling out forms. Look them up in your telephone directory to find out the opening times and if it is possible to make an appointment.

The Disability Alliance produces a 'Disability Rights Handbook' which covers benefits available to people with disabilities and their families.

Disability Alliance
Universal House
88-94 Wentworth Street
London E1 7SA
020 7247 8776
www.disabilityalliance.org.uk

The Family Fund
Unit 4 Alpha Court
Monks Cross Drive
Huntington
York Y32 9WN
0845 130 4542
info@familyfund.org.uk
www.familyfund.org.uk

MENCAP
123 Golden Lane
London EC1Y ORT
020 7454 0454
www.mencap.org.uk

Learning Disability Helpline: 0808 808 1111 (Mon-Fri 10-4)

Benefit Enquiry Line for people with disabilities and their carers: 0800 882200 (freephone).

4

EDUCATION

Your child's education will undoubtedly play an extremely important part in his/her life, as not only will s/he be spending many hours a week in school for many years, but it is how s/he gets on at school that will determine very much how s/he is out of school. It is therefore important that you know as much as possible about the options open to your son or daughter so that s/he is happy at school and has his or her potential developed to the full.

This chapter outlines some of the options for pre-school education, and then discusses the formal assessment of children with disabilities and/or special needs, and the document which often follows an assessment, which is called a statement or the process of statementing. Other education jargon, such as the Code of Practice under the Education Act 1996 and The Special Educational Needs and Disability Act 2001, will be explained as well as a brief exploration of the debate between integration and segregation of disabled children in the education system.

Pre-school education
Whatever the extent of your child's disability, s/he will be helped by some pre-school education to prepare him or her for full-time school and to help him or her develop to his or her full potential. Opportunities for pre-school learning for your child include portage, playgroups, day nurseries and nursery classes.

Portage

Portage is a home-based learning programme which can commence as early as when your child is only a few months old. Portage, which has already been described in chapter 2, is a very important source of pre-school education and can be invaluable in teaching your child new skills. Apart from asking your G.P., Paediatrician or health visitor about portage, you could contact the National Portage Association UK for details of local schemes (see the end of this chapter for the address and telephone number).

Playgroups

Playgroups and opportunity groups can help your child develop socially by mixing with other young children and through play. Ask your health visitor and/or the Pre-school Learning Alliance (address at end of chapter) for playgroups which are available in your area.

Day Nurseries and children's centres

Day nurseries are usually run privately. Childcare in children's centres, which integrate health, social care and education for under fives, is increasingly available and are run by sure start and local authority children's services departments. Remember that disabled children have an entitlement to some day care under both the Children Act 1989 and the Childcare Act 2006. Ask your local authority social services or children's services departments for advice or contact Childcare Link freephone on 08000 96 02 96 or visit www.childcarelink.org.uk .

Nursery Classes

Unfortunately there are few nursery class places throughout the country. However, if your child is recognised as having special educational needs from an early age, s/he may be entitled to high priority for a nursery place. Ask your Local Education Authority about the schools you should approach.

Peripatetic Teachers

It also may be possible for the Local Education Authority to arrange a Peripatetic Teacher to visit you and your child at home, depending on whether this service is available in your area. Some of these teachers may specialise in hearing or visual impairments, or both.

Assessment of special education needs

Children have their special education needs assessed if they have learning difficulties and need special help. A child has learning difficulties if s/he finds it much harder to learn than most children of the same age, or if s/he has a disability which makes it difficult to use the ordinary education facilities in the area.

Pre-school

If your child has not received a specific diagnosis or recognition from the medical profession that his or her development is delayed, and s/he has not yet started school and you are concerned that s/he may need specialist help, you need to talk to a professional such as a doctor, health visitor etc. Or you can talk to the Local Education Authority (LEA) directly instead for advice. The phone number of the LEA will be in your telephone directory under your local council. You can ask your LEA to make a statutory assessment of his or her special educational needs. The LEA must then make a statutory assessment, unless they decide it is unnecessary.

If your child has been diagnosed as having a condition or disability from a young age, a health professional will probably refer him or her directly to the LEA, after consulting you. They will discuss his or her needs with you and look at how best s/he may be helped. The LEA will then decide whether it is necessary to make a statutory assessment.

At School

If your child has already started school and you are concerned that s/he has learning difficulties, you need to talk to your child's teacher or head teacher. At the school there will be someone who has special responsibility for children with special educational needs - the Special Needs Coordinator (SENCO) - who you then need to talk to.

Under the Education Act 1996, and the Special Educational Needs and Disability Act 2001, which came into force in January 2002, schools are expected to publish information about their policies for children with special educational needs (SEN) and have regard to what's called a Code of Practice on the **Identification and Assessment of SEN.**

The Special Educational Needs Code of Practice gives guidance to early education settings, state schools and local education authorities. It sets out the processes and procedures that all these organisations must or should follow to meet the needs of children. The Code of Practice must not be ignored. A copy of this Code is available free of charge from the Department for Education and Skills (DfES) Publications Centre (0845 6022260).

The Code describes how help for children with special educational needs in schools and early education settings should be made by a step-by-step or 'graduated approach'. Stages within the Code of Practice are followed before making a statutory assessment of your child's special educational needs. These are outlined below.

Stages of the Special Educational Needs Code of Practice
The Code recommends that schools should deal with a child's needs step-by-step or in stages. Your child will only move from one step to another if it is seen as necessary. Early education settings and schools place great importance on identifying special educational needs early so that they can help children as quickly as possible. You should be consulted at each stage.

Stage One – Early Years Action or School Action

The school must tell you when they first start giving your child extra help, such as small group work or one-to-one. Your child's teacher should record any concerns about your child's learning difficulty and should speak to you about them. A full discussion of your child's needs, and any relevant history of your child's difficulties, should take place at this stage.

Stage Two – Individual Education Plan (IEP)

The teacher responsible for special educational needs (SENCO) should talk to you and your child's other teachers and should draw up an individual education plan. This plan sets targets for your child to achieve and a date for a review of his or her progress. The school may ask you to work with your child and to help him or her at home.

Stage Three – Early Years Action Plus or School Action Plus

At this stage, the school is likely to look for some specialist help or advice from outside the school, such as from a Speech and Language Therapist, Educational Psychologist or Specialist Teacher. A new individual education plan will be drawn up. You will be kept informed about your child's progress and invited to all review meetings. If your child is not making enough progress, the Head teacher will decide whether to ask the LEA to make a statutory assessment. Throughout all the stages, you have a right to take part in decisions about your child's education. Your views are very important.

The Statutory Assessment

This is a very detailed examination of what your child's special educational needs are and all the special help s/he may need. Your views are very important and you should be involved in the whole process.

If the LEA decide to make a statutory assessment of your child, they need to tell you within 6 weeks. Sometimes the LEA will decide that your child's needs can be met in his or her present school and do not make a statutory assessment. If you disagree with this you have a right to appeal to the Special Educational Needs Tribunal.

When a statutory assessment takes place, detailed information is collected from your child's school, his or her doctor, an Education Psychologist and most importantly ,you, his or her parent(s). You have an essential part to play because you know your child better then anyone else.

The LEA should give you information about the different types of special help that ordinary and special schools in your area can offer. You can then visit some of these schools to decide which you might like your child to attend. You may feel that you want independent advice when your child's needs are being assessed and discussed.

To help you, you are entitled to support from your local *parent partnership service*. This service should be able to give you advice and information as well as emotional support. Ask your LEA about the parent partnership service.

After the assessment is complete, a decision will be made by the LEA whether to make a statement of special educational needs for your child. The LEA should let you know this within 12 weeks of starting the assessment.

Statements of special educational needs
A statement of special educational needs is a document that sets out your child's needs and all the special help s/he should have.

A statement of special educational needs is in 6 parts:

Part One: -gives your own and your child's name and address and other details.

Part Two: -gives details of all your child's learning difficulties and disabilities as identified by the LEA during the assessment.

Part Three: -describes

> - all the special help that the LEA think your child should get to meet the needs set out in Part Two;
> - the long-term objectives to be achieved by that special help; and
> - the arrangements to be made for setting short-term targets and regularly reviewing your child's progress towards those targets.

Part Four: - tells you about the school where your child will go to get the special help set out in Part three, or the arrangements for education to be made otherwise than at school.

Part Five: - describes any non-educational needs your child has, such as transport to school.

Part Six: - describes how your child will get the help described in Part five.

Normally it is the Principal Education Psychologist in your area who will prepare the final statement but views should be sought from professionals involved with your child as well as you, the parents. The professionals consulted are likely to include health professionals such as your G.P., Consultant, Physiotherapist, Occupational Therapist, a Social Worker and teaching staff.

Before the LEA sends you the final statement, they will send you a 'proposed statement'. This includes all parts except part 4. With this the LEA will then send you a letter telling you how you can give your views on the proposed statement before it is finalised.

The LEA will also send you details of state ordinary schools and state special schools in your area. You have a right to express a preference for which state school you want your child to go to. However, the LEA must agree with your preference as long as:

(i)　the school you choose is suitable for your child's age, ability and special educational needs;

(ii)　your child's presence there will not affect the education of other children already at the school; and

(iii)　placing your child in the school will be an efficient use of the LEA's resources.

Clearly then, it is quite easy for the LEA to argue against your preference if they see fit. It is important therefore for you to collect as much evidence as possible to demonstrate that your child would be better off in a particular school. The Advisory Centre for Education (see address at the end of this chapter) can offer advice and support to parents whose children are going through the statementing process. Other useful organisations are listed both at the end of this chapter and the book.

After the LEA have sent you the proposed statement, you have 15 days to reply to comment and say which school you would like your child to attend. You can ask for a meeting with the LEA to discuss the proposed statement after which you have another 15 days to send in more comments or request another meeting. Usually the LEA should make the final statement within 8 weeks of the proposed statement.

If you disagree with what is in the statement, you should ask an officer at your LEA for an explanation. If you are still not happy, you have a right to appeal to the Special Educational Needs Tribunal against the contents of part 2, 3 or 4 of the statement. There is more about the Tribunal and what to do if you disagree, in chapter 8.

Once the statement is in place, it must be reviewed at least once a year. The school will do this by holding a review, to which you will be invited to attend. This annual review may lead to changes to your child's statement if his or her needs have changed, the LEA have decided that different kinds of extra help are necessary or if your child has to move to a different school. You will be asked for your views before changes are made.

A child's statement may last for all of his or her school life or just part of it, depending on his or her needs and progress. These will be discussed at reviews.

Segregation versus integration in education
The arguments for and against disabled children being educated in mainstream (ordinary) schools or in special schools have been debated fiercely by parents and educationalists over many years.

Special school education means segregated education. Special schools are often a long way from a child's home and therefore separated from his or her local community and peers. Once the child has reached the age of 19, s/he will need, in most cases, to return to his or her local community, from which s/he has been separated for many years. Special schools in the main will emphasise the learning of social skills and independent living skills rather than academic achievement.

However, special schools are favoured by many people because it is at these schools that disabled children have greater access to the services they need, such as physiotherapy, speech therapy and occupational therapy. They will also have specialised teaching equipment and specially trained teachers.

Sometimes when disabled children attend ordinary mainstream schools, they can be over-protected or treated as special because of their disability. This will depend on the school and how the issues of disability and integration are approached by the teaching staff and the ethos of the establishment. However, if this type of treatment of a disabled child does go on, the school is not equipping him or her for independence. Some parents fear the teasing or bullying their child may be subjected to in a mainstream school, or that their child will not be able to keep up with the others.

Other parents and educationalists believe that integration is the answer to equal educational and social opportunities to children who have special educational needs. Attending a mainstream school, it is argued, means that disabled children can grow up within a 'real life' community, can develop out-of-school relationships in his or her local area, will do better academically and will also help those non-disabled children understand the concept of disability and view it more positively.

In many areas, though, both special schools and mainstream schools are pursuing integration policies, by mixing classes from different schools on a regular basis and by having a special unit attached to a mainstream school, for example. It is important for you to be aware of what's available in your local area, so ask your LEA for information as early as possible.

The Special Educational Needs and Disability Act 2001 places an emphasis on the inclusion of children with special educational needs. It says that the special educational needs of children will normally be met in mainstream schools as long as other children's education is not adversely affected and parents are in agreement. Part 2 of the Act, which came into force in September 2002, extends disability discrimination to cover schools. There is now a duty on schools not to treat students with disabilities any less favourably than non-disabled students in school life.

KEY POINTS

- Pre-school education, such as Portage, playgroups, day nurseries/children's centers, nursery classes, is important for your child. Ask your G.P., health visitor or other professional.

- Special educational needs means having learning difficulties and needing extra help at school.

- If your child needs his or her special educational needs assessed before s/he is 5, this will be started by a health professional or yourself asking the Local Education Authority (LEA).

- If your child is assessed whilst s/he is already at school, Stages 1 to 3 of the Code of Practice will be followed before a statutory assessment starts.

- After the assessment, your child may be statemented. A statement is a document that sets out your child's needs and all the special help s/he should have.

- If you disagree with any actions of the LEA, you should talk to them or your child's school first. If you are still unhappy, you can appeal to the Special Educational Needs Tribunal. There is more about this in chapter 8.

- There are many arguments for and against educating disabled children in special or mainstream schools. In the end, what's decided for your child will be based on your views and the views of the LEA about your child's needs. As far as possible, your child's own views and wishes should be taken into account. Find out all the options as early as possible. Some of the organisations listed below may be able to help.

USEFUL ORGANISATIONS

DFES (Department for Education and Skills)
Sanctuary Buildings
Great Smith Street
London SW1P 3BT
0870 000 2288 (Monday-Friday 9-5)
www. dfes.gov.uk

Publishes guidance on education and provides leaflets for parents. Website has a section designed specifically for parents.

Advisory Centre for Education (ACE)
1b Aberdeen Studios
22 Highbury Grove
London N5 2EA
0808 800 5793 (freephone advice line. Monday-Friday 2-5 pm)
www.ace-ed.org.uk

Offers guidance and advice on all aspects of education. Has publications and produces a Special Education Handbook.

Independent Panel for Special Education Advice (IPSEA)
6 Carlow Mews
Woodbridge
Suffolk IP12 1DH
0800 018 4016 (advice line)
www.ipsea.org.uk

Independent experts who give advice to parents who are uncertain about or disagree with the local education authority's views of the child's special educational needs.

Parents for Inclusion
Unit 1, Winchester House
Kennington Park Business Centre
Cranmer Street
London SW9 6EJ
020 7735 7735 (office)

info@parentsforinclusion.org
www.parentsforinclusion.org

(Inclusion helpline open Mon, Tues, Thurs 10-12 and 1-3)

Centre for Studies on Inclusive Education (CSIE)
Room 2S 203, S Block, Frenchay Campus
Coldharbour Lane
Bristol BS16 1QU
0117 3444007
www.inclusion.uwe.ac.uk/csie/

Information available on the education of children with special needs within mainstream schools.

Network 81
1-7 Woodfield Terrace
Chapel Hill
Stansted
Essex CM24 8AJ
0870 770 3262

0870 770 3306 (helpline open Monday to Friday 10-2)

info@network81.org
www.network81.co.uk

Gives advice on education assessments, statementing and special educational provision.

National Portage Association UK
127 Monk's Dale
Yeovil
Somerset BA21 3JE
01935 471641
www.portage.org.uk

Pre-school Learning Alliance
The Fitzpatrick Building
188 York Way
London N7 9AD

020 7697 2500

Helpline: 020 7837 5513
www.pre-school.org.uk

National Association for the Education of Sick Children
18 Victoria Park Square, Bethnal Green, London E2 OPF
020 8980 8523
www.sickhildren.org.uk

National Association of Special Educational Needs
4-5 Amber Business Village, Amker Close, Tamworth B77 4RP
01827 311500
www.nasen.org.uk

5

BREAKS AND HOLIDAYS

We all need breaks from our everyday routine, whether this is working full-time or caring for someone, or both. Having a breathing space from caring for a disabled child is no exception so try not to feel guilty about it. To make sure you can care for your child as best as you can, you will need time to yourself, with your partner and your other children. Remember too that your disabled child is likely to enjoy the opportunity of doing new things with other children and adults and will probably learn much from the experience. Breaks away with your child are also important and there are now many organisations which can help you plan a holiday with your disabled child.

This chapter outlines some of the possibilities for short-term breaks or respite care, such as family based schemes, play schemes or residential care, and holidays, and lists some organisations which may be of use to you.

Respite breaks or short term breaks

Respite care or the newer term - short-term breaks - is often used to describe the situation when a child goes away from the family home overnight to give his or her parent/carer a break. This is misleading as respite care or short-term breaks can also apply to care given to a child in his or her own home whilst the parent/carer goes out, and to short-term breaks during the day, such as play schemes.

Many parents find it very hard to part with their child even when they really need the break, and for a relatively short space of time.

You may feel like this and guilty about leaving the care of your child in the hands of someone else who isn't a member of your family or a close friend. This is understandable but can be overcome by planning respite care so that you and your child can get to know someone over a space of time before you leave them in charge of your child. Because respite care may be needed in an emergency - if you were taken ill, for example, and there was no one else to care for your child - is it important for you to check out the respite care possibilities at an early stage before any crisis may occur.

Some of the different types of respite care or short-term breaks are listed and described below.

Family Based Respite Care

Family based respite care schemes are usually run by local voluntary agencies or by social services departments. They assess, recruit, train and monitor single people or families who are able to look after a disabled child in their home on a regular basis, like 1 night a fortnight, a weekend per month, or sometimes longer spells like a week or a fortnight on occasions (e.g. once/twice a year) so the parent(s) can go away.

The procedure for recruiting, assessing and approving carers is very thorough and governed by Children Act 1989 guidelines, and is very similar to the procedure for recruiting foster parents. So you can rest assured from the start that the carer matched to your child is as suitable and capable as possible. Remember too that the person, and any other adult in the same household, would have been checked against Police and social services records. Although this, unfortunately, does not guarantee that the person would not abuse your child in any way, it makes it much less likely.

The scheme who recruits carers for a disabled child will have information about you and your child, what s/he is like, what his or her disabilities are and what his or her likes and dislikes are. They will then match you and your child with a carer they judge to be suitable for your child. They will try and match racial, cultural and religious backgrounds as far as possible. It is then usual for you and your child to meet with the prospective carer and his or her own family on several occasions, at your home and the carer's home, to get to know each other. Only after a few meetings will it be possible for your child to stay overnight at the carer's home.

Family based respite care does not always have to mean overnight care though. Many carers are willing and able to take care of children during the day during the week on occasions (during the school holidays occasionally, for example) or sometimes at the weekend. This can normally be negotiated with the carer and who ever is running the scheme.

Family based respite care schemes tend to work well for both parents and children. Consequently, this means that the schemes that do exist are over-stretched, resulting in long waiting lists. Try and find out what's available in your local area at an early stage, by asking your social services department or voluntary agency.

Residential Respite Care

Residential respite care units for disabled children are run by health, social services or voluntary agencies. They offer overnight care for your child on an emergency or regular basis, if you meet certain criteria which varies depending on the unit. If you are able to plan your child's first stay, it is best to visit the unit with your child to meet some of the staff and look around the facilities. This will mean that parting from your child and seeing your child go away from home will be much easier for you both. You can find out about what residential respite care is available by asking your health professional, social services department or voluntary agency. It is worth noting that it is not always easy to obtain such care - you need to demonstrate the importance of it for both you and your child. Getting support from a sympathetic professional may also be helpful.

Play schemes and After School Clubs

Plays schemes for the school holidays and after school clubs are normally run by the leisure department of your local council, although some are also run by voluntary agencies. They are normally based in schools and offer play activities and outings in a relaxed but supervised environment.

Your child may be able to join the play schemes and clubs run for non-disabled children, depending on what his or her needs are. Special schemes and clubs are also run for disabled children. Ask your leisure department, social services or local voluntary organisation for more information.

Respite Care or Short-term Breaks in Your Home

Many parents feel guilty about taking up respite care opportunities as it feels like they are sending their child away from home. First, many children enjoy this break themselves and learn new things and meet new people whilst away and second, there may also be opportunities for respite care in your home meaning that your child can stay at home whilst you go out.

This type of respite care, however, is not normally for overnights. Such breaks will usually be for care during the day, such as 2-4 hours, to give you time to go shopping, see some friends, or simply spend some time alone or with your partner.

One of the main national organisations offering this type of care is the Crossroads Caring for Carer schemes across the country, and they employ carers who go into families once a week for 4 hours or twice a week for 2 hours. Most families receive a maximum of 4 hours per week but this depends on their needs and circumstances. Carers work all hours so it is possible to have help at weekends and evenings as well as during the day. Crossroads carers work with children and people of all ages and all disabilities.

Some local Crossroads Caring for Carers schemes also offer an occasional night sitting service if your sleep is often interrupted.

Some areas may not have a Crossroads Caring for Carers scheme but will have a similar scheme which works under a different name. Ask the Crossroads Caring for Carers national organisation (address at the end of this chapter) or your local social services department, health professional or voluntary organisation to see if you have a local scheme.

Holidays

Having a disabled child should not mean that you cannot go away. There are many organisations that can help you plan a holiday with your child or who can organise an independent trip for him or her if s/he is old enough.

The following organisations publish information about holidays for the disabled including family holidays, activity holidays and holidays for unaccompanied disabled children and adults.

Holiday Care
0845 124 9971 (Mon-Tues 9-5;Wed-Fri 9-1)

www.holidaycare.org.uk

RADAR (Royal Association for Disability and Rehabilitation)
12 City Forum
250 City Road
London EC1V 8AF
020 7250 3222
www.radar.org.uk

Disabled Holiday Directory
6 Seaview Cresent
Goodwick SA64 OAT
01348 875592
www.disabledholidaydirectory.co.uk

Learning Disability Helpline
0808 808 1111

The following organisations can provide holidays and holiday accommodation for disabled children and their families. This is only a small selection of the full list, which can be obtained from RADAR. The Learning Disability Helpline also has a very comprehensive list.

Break
1 Montague Road
Sheringham NR26 8LN

01263 822161
www.break-charity.org

Specialises in holidays for multiply disabled children and adults, individuals, groups and those unaccompanied by parents or staff.

Across Trust
Bridge House
70-72 Bridge Road
East Molesey
Surrey KT8 9HF

020 8783 1355

Organises holidays for disabled people of all ages across Europe in fully equipped Jumbulances.

THE CALVERT TRUST
Keilder
Keilder Water

Hexham
Northumberland NE48 1BS
01434 250232
www.calvert-trust.org.uk/kielder

KESWICK
Little Crosthwaite
Keswick
Cumbria CA12 4QD
017687 72254
www.calvert-trust.keswick

EXMOOR
Wislandpound Farm
Kentisbury
North Devon EX31 4SJ
01598 763221
www.calvert-trust.org.uk/exmoor
The Calvert Trust in Northumberland, Cumbria and Devon have purpose built centres for disabled people and their families offering a wide range of sports and recreational activities.

3H Fund (Help the Handicapped Holiday Fund)
147a Camden Road
Tunbridge Wells
TN1 2RA
01892 547474
www.3hfund.org.uk

Group holidays for physically disabled children and young people over 11 years.

National Holiday Fund for Sick and Disabled Children
PO Box 44

Belvedere
DA17 6WT
01341 280 486

www.nhfcharity.co.uk

Provides holidays to Florida for chronically or terminally ill children and physically disabled children, between the ages of 8 and 18. Grants are not available.

FINANCING HOLIDAYS
Social Services/children's services
Disabled children and their families may be able to obtain a small grant from their social services department towards a holiday. The criteria for receiving some funding will vary from one council to another, but many means test and/or will only give money to a family every few years.

Charitable Organisations

ADCARE HOLIDAY FUND
The Holiday Fund Administrator
The Membership Office
Mencap National Centre
123 Golden Lane
London EC1Y ORT
020 2454 0454
Email: holidayfund@mencap.org.uk

Provides grants towards the cost of a holiday for individuals with learning disabilities.

THE FAMILY FUND
Unit 4, Alpha Court
Monks Cross Drive
Huntington
York Y32 9WN

0845 130 4542
www.familyfund.org.uk
info@familyfund.org.uk

To receive funding, there must be a severely disabled child under the age of 16 in the family. Grants vary in size and can be used towards family holidays with or without the disabled child.

THE FAMILY HOLIDAY ASSOCIATION
16 Mortimer Street
London W1T 3JL
020 7436 3304
www.fhaonline.org.uk
The Family Holiday Association provides grants for families for one week's holiday of their choice. The family must be referred to the Association by social services, health professional or local voluntary organization. The child must be at least 3 years old.

PEARSON'S HOLIDAY FUND
P.O. Box 3017
South Croydon
CR2 9PN
020 8657 3053
www.pearsonsholidayfund.org.uk
Funds children aged 4-17 whilst on holiday in the U.K. The fund only deals with the referrer, i.e. the doctor, social worker, health visitor etc, rather than the family.

FAMILY WELFARE ASSOCIATION
501-505 Kingsland Road
London E8 4AU
020 7254 6251

www.fwa.org.uk

Provides grants for holidays to families with disabled children. Applications are made through social services or health professional.

More information on financing holidays can be obtained from RADAR and the Holiday Care Service. See section on useful reading for more details.

KEY POINTS

- You may feel guilty about needing a break from your child. This is perfectly understandable but remember that we all need breaks from our everyday routine and caring responsibilities.

- Respite care or short term breaks does covers a variety of possibilities: family based schemes, residential respite care, play schemes, after school clubs and care within the home whilst you go out.

- It is not always easy to obtain respite care, so find out about opportunities in your local area from an early stage. It is also always best to plan respite care and meet the person or people who will be caring for your child, so try and apply for respite care before any sort of crisis occurs.

- Having a holiday with your disabled child is also important. There are many organisations which can help you do this, which are listed above. Holidays can also be arranged for your child to go away on his or her own, if s/he is old enough.

USEFUL ORGANISATIONS

CROSSROADS CARING FOR CARERS
10 Regent Place
Rugby
Warwickshire
CV21 2PN
0845 450 0350
www.crossroads.org.uk

SHARED CARE NETWORK(Association to promote family based short-term care)
63-66 Easton Business Centre
Felix Road
Easton
Bristol BS5 OHE
0117 9415361
www.sharedcarenetwork.org.uk

HOLIDAY CARE
0845 124 9971 (Mon-Tues 9-5; Wed-Fri 9-1)
www.holidayare.org.uk

RADAR
12 City Forum
250 City Road
London EC1V 8AF
020 7250 3222
www.radar.org.uk

6

TRANSPORT AND EQUIPMENT

Help with transport and equipment for your disabled child is designed to make life a little easier for both you and your son or daughter, and can assist both with getting around and encouraging independence. It is best to know what the options are, therefore, which this chapter aims to do by outlining some of the main sources of help with transport and equipment. For more detailed advice about equipment to help your child be as independent as possible, both inside and outside the home, it is advisable to talk to an Occupational Therapist, who can be found in the health service or social services.

FINANCIAL HELP WITH TRANSPORT

Welfare Benefits
This has been dealt with in chapter 3 and covers the following areas relevant to this section:
(i)   fares to hospital
(ii)   road tax exemption
(iii)   mobility component of the Disabled Living Allowance (DLA)
(iv)   social fund

Use this list to make sure you are getting everything you and your child are entitled to.

Family Fund

To receive any help from the Family Fund a family must have a severely disabled child under the age of 16. Please see chapter 3 for more details. To help with transport costs, a child must only be receiving the lower rate of the mobility component of DLA. The Family Fund sometimes agrees to pay for driving lessons for parents.

HELP WITH CAR USE

Buying a Car - Motability

Motability is both a private company and registered charity, which receives a government grant to cover its administrative costs. It helps disabled people or the families of disabled children, who receive the higher rate of the mobility component of DLA, to lease a new car or to buy a new or second-hand car or a powered wheelchair on hire purchase.

For more details of the scheme, contact Motability direct. The address and telephone number is listed at the end of this chapter.

Parking - the Blue European Parking Badge

This scheme has recently replaced the orange badge, which enabled disabled people as drivers or passengers or the parents of disabled children to park on a yellow line for up to 2 hours (as long as they are not causing an obstruction) in England and Wales, and without a time limit in Scotland and park without charge or time limit on parking meters. This does not apply in central London.

To qualify, you need to show that you or your child has a permanent and substantial disability which causes very considerable difficulty in walking, which has to be verified by your G.P. or Consultant, or be in receipt of the higher rate of the mobility component of the Disability Living Allowance, or who is registered blind. To obtain a blue badge, you need to apply to your local social services office.

PUBLIC TRANSPORT

Travel Permits for Buses and Trains

Many local councils offer travel permits for children and young people who are disabled and over the age of 5. The criteria and availability will vary from one council to another but generally, being in receipt of the higher rate of mobility component of DLA is enough to qualify automatically. If your child does not receive this, your child's G.P. will probably be asked for information to support the application. Ask your local social services office for more details.

Taxicards

A number of local councils offer concessions on the cost of taxi fares. Again, this will vary from one council to another. The critera will be similar to that of the Blue Badge and the travel permit. Ask your local social services office for more details.

Community transport schemes

Some areas offer cheap transport for people with mobility problems. The names and details of the schemes will vary from one area to another. Ask you local voluntary agency for the disabled or Citizens Advice Bureau for more information.

More information about how you can be helped with transport can be found in leaflets and publications which are listed in the 'Useful Reading' section of this book.

Equipment

Generally, it is very important that your child has a proper assessment for any equipment s/he needs, by a qualified professional such as an Occupational Therapist or Physiotherapist through social services or the hospital s/he attends.

Buggies and Wheelchairs

If your child has serious problems with walking and is over 2 1/2 years old, you should be able to get him or her a buggy or wheelchair from your local Wheelchair Centre. In Scotland and Wales these are called Artificial Limb and Appliance Centres. In Northern Ireland they are called Prosthetic and Orthotic Aids Centres.

If your child is under 2 1/2 years old, has serious difficulties with walking amd has special seating needs, s/he may still be able to get this help.

Ask your child's GP, hospital specialist, Occupational Therapist to refer your child to the Wheelchair Centre.

Nappies and Incontinence Aids

Once a child is over the age of infancy but is still incontinent as a result of a disability, your local health authority can provide a supply of incontinence aids. These include disposable nappies and pads, bed pads and plastic pants.

Ask your G.P, Community Paediatrician, Health Visitor or School Nurse for advice.

Adaptations to Housing

If your child has a physical disability, it may be necessary to adapt your accommodation. It is advisable to plan ahead as early as possible because it takes a long time to find out what adaptations are necessary and possible and how they will be financed.

It is sometimes possible to receive financial help for adaptations under the Disabled Facilities Grants from your local council. The schemes vary from one area to another, but are always means-tested, so you need to check with your local council what can be offered.

As a first step, you need to talk to an Occupational Therapist at your Social Services Department.

Further information can be obtained from RADAR.

Now read the key points overleaf.

KEY POINTS

- For financial help with transport, you may be entitled to one of the following benefits: social fund help, fares to hospital, mobility component of the DLA, road tax exemption or help from the Family Fund.

- If your child has problems with his or her mobility, you may be eligible for help in obtaining a car through the motability scheme, blue badge for concessions in parking, a travel permit for your child and/or a taxicard.

- Help with equipment such as wheelchairs and other adaptations to your house may be obtained through an Occupational Therapist in the first instance.

USEFUL ORGANISATIONS

MOTABILITY OPERATIONS
City Gate House
22 Southwark Bridge Road
London SE1 9HB
0845 456 4566
www.motability.co.uk

RADAR
12 City Forum
250 City Road
London EC1V 8AF
020 7250 3222
www.radar.org.uk

DISABLED LIVING FOUNDATION
380-384 Harrow Road
London W9 2HU
Helpline: 0845 130 9177 (Mon-Fri 10-4)

www.dlf.org.uk
Gives advice about equipment and all aspects of disabled living.

THE DISABILITY INFORMATION TRUST
Mary Marlborough Centre
Nuffield Orthopaedic Centre
Headington
Oxford OX3 7LD
01865 227592

www.abilityonline.org.uk

WHIZZ-KIDZ
Eliot House
10-12 Allington Street
London SW1E 5EH
020 7233 6600
www.whizz-kidz.org.uk

Provides mobility equipment to disabled children under 18 years of age. Aims to help disabled children have improved mobility, increased independence and a better quality of life.

ASSOCIATION OF WHEELCHAIR CHILDREN
6 Woodman Parade
North Woolwich
London E16 2LL
0870 121 0050
www.wheelchairchildren.org.uk

Provides advice, equipment and training to children who use wheelchairs.

Kids (National Office)
6 Aztec Row
Berners Road
London N1 OPW

enquiries@kids.org.uk
www.kids-online.org.uk

Promotes play opportunities for disabled children.

7

TOWARDS ADULTHOOD

The transition from childhood to adulthood is a period of change for all young people and their families, and being a disabled young person is no exception to this rule.

It is during the teenage years that services change for a disabled young person, future opportunities for education, training, work and living need to be looked into, new welfare benefits become available and the young person becomes independent, not least in the area of sexuality and relationships. This period can be a difficult time for parents, who may still feel very protective towards their son or daughter and can find it hard to accept that s/he is growing up and growing away, especially if s/he is disabled and is, in some ways, still dependent. All these issues will be addressed in this chapter.

Welfare benefits at age 16
Once a disabled young person reaches the age of 16, s/he can claim benefits, regardless of his or her parents' income or savings. There are three main benefits for the over 16s, who are disabled: Incapacity Benefit (which has replaced Severe Disablement Allowance), Disability Living Allowance (DWA) and Income Support. The young person may also be eligible for disability premiums, which are added to Income Support.

Incapacity Benefit
Although Incapacity Benefit is dependent on the payment of national contributions, if the young person is under 20, they may be still able get Incapacity Benefit, even if they have not paid any

national insurance. In addition, if the young person is over 20 but under 25 and was in education or training immediately before their 20th birthday, they also may be able to get Incapacity Benefit even if they have not paid enough national contributions.

To apply for Incapacity Benefit ask for a form from your local Social Security Office or telephone the Benefit Enquiry line free on 0800 882200 or 0800 243355 (minicom).

Income Support
Income Support can be claimed on its own or to "top up" Incapacity Benefit. The "top up ", ie. the disability premium, is about £23 per week. Anyone receiving DLA (Care) at the higher or middle rate or who is registered blind, automatically qualifies for the disability premium.

Young people receiving Income Support who have extra needs caused by their disability, such as extra clothing, bedding or laundry equipment, may apply to the Social Fund for a Community Care Grant, although any savings of £500 or more will be deducted from the grant. Remember that Incapacity Benefit and Income Support may be claimed while still at school or in further education. Parents should note, however, that if your son or daughter applies for Income Support in his or her own right, you will lose your Child Benefit and premiums for having dependent children, such as Lone Parent premium. You will also have to sign on for work unless you are getting Carer's Allowance.

Housing Benefit
People aged 16 or over with less than £16,000 savings who pay rent or service charges where they live may be able to get Housing Benefit. Please note that no help is available towards charges paid to close relatives, such as parents. The arrangements must be 'commercial', for example with a landlord, housing association or local council.

To claim housing benefit apply to your local council housing department for a claim form.

Direct Payments

Once disabled young people reach the age of 16, they may be able to arrange and buy in their own care with money paid to them by social services departments. These are called direct payments. Your social services departments will be able to give more information about this scheme. The independent living fund, which is described further in this chapter, can also give money to buy personal care.

Education and training

When your child/young person reaches the age of 14, a reassessment of his or her special educational needs must be made. This should include a 'Transition Plan' which aims to co-ordinate plans for the young person's transition from child to adult services and should include an assessment by the Social Services Department of needs other than educational ones.

Compulsory education ends at age 16 but this does not mean the end of full-time education. All young people have a legal right to education until their 19th birthday. Well before your son or daughter's 16th birthday, it is important to look at the possibility of continuing education after the age of 16, either at his or her present school or at other local schools or colleges of further education. Youth training schemes may also be able to offer your son or daughter vocational training. People who will be able to help you look into these opportunities are school staff, a A Connexions Personal Advisor and organisations such as Skill and RADAR (addresses at the end of this chapter).

Work opportunities
Ordinary Employment

Some disabled young people are able to enter ordinary employment soon after leaving school, college or Youth Training. There are several schemes to increase employment opportunities for people with disabilities, including financial help towards the cost of getting to and from work, if the young person cannot use public transport and the loaning of special equipment or modified equipment to disabled employees.

The Connexions service will be able to advise on ordinary employment opportunities for your young person. Remember too that if s/he finds a part-time job of more than 16 hours per week, s/he may be able to get Disability Persons Tax Credit to top up a low wage.

Connexions is the government's support service for all young people aged 13-19 in England. The service aims to provide integrated advice, guidance and access to personal development opportunities, including information and advice on courses and careers, and to help them make a smooth transition to adulthood and working life. All young people will have access to a personal advisor. For some young people, this will just be for careers advice; for others – including for disabled young people – it may involve more in depth support to help identify barriers to learning and get more specialist support, the Personal Advisors do outreach work and work in schools, colleges and community centers.

There are some specialist schemes to help disabled young people to get and keep an ordinary job, such as the Pathway Scheme run by MENCAP. Contact MENCAP to see if such a scheme is run in your area.

Sheltered Employment
Sheltered employment is aimed specifically at people with severe disabilities, both physical and learning, who are unlikely to get an ordinary job in open employment. Jobs include work such as packing, gardening, laundry or furniture-making. Sheltered employment is provided in workshops and factories by Remploy

(address at the end of this chapter) local authorities and voluntary agencies.

The Sheltered Employment Scheme enables severely disabled people to work in open, ordinary employment alongside other non-disabled people, with support from a sponsoring body. For more details on all of these opportunities, ask the specialist careers officer at your local Careers Service or the Disability Employment Adviser at your local Job Centre.

Day Centres

Adult training centres (ATCs), or social education centres, are run by social services departments for people with learning disabilities. They offer job training and work experience; basic education; arts and craft work; independent living skills, such as using public transport, shopping, home management; and leisure and recreational activities.

Day centres also exist for young people with physical disabilities. They may offer similar activities and industrial work and job training.

Transport is normally provided for attendance at day centres and attendance can often be combined with a course at a local college

To arrange a place at a day centre, you should discuss the possibility with your son or daughter's school and with the specialist careers officer. You could also ask a social worker at your local social services department office.

Accommodation
Independent Living

Specially adapted homes for people with physical disabilities can be provided by local authority housing departments and housing associations. If someone needs a considerable amount of care to live independently because they have physical and/or learning disabilities, it may be possible to obtain live in care from Community Service Volunteers through their Independent Living Schemes. There are also several types of care attendant schemes, where a helper visits regularly during the day and evening. Schemes may be run by the Crossroads Caring for Carers schemes or the Leonard Cheshire Foundation Family Support Service. There are also some local authority care schemes. Ask your social service department for more details. You will need to see someone from the team working with adults with disabilities.

Independent Living Fund

The Independent Living Fund (0845 601 8815 www.ilf.org.uk) can give a disabled person money to buy extra care services on top of the services or direct payments they receive from social services. It exists to assist with the costs of domiciliary and personal care to live in their own homes rather than going into care and is available to people aged 16 and 65. An application has to be made through social services.

Residential Provision

Living in a residential home with other young people with disabilities may be a more suitable option for those people who need more care, help and supervision.

Residential homes are run by social services departments, housing associations and other voluntary agencies, such as MENCAP. Contact your social services office and voluntary agency to see what is available in your area.

You can also contact CARESEARCH (0800 380 2077) to find suitable residential care. They will take the details of the young person and their needs and then match them up to suitable homes, for which a small charge is made.

There are also a number of voluntary organisations throughout the country which provide long-term accommodation.

Bear in mind, however, that these homes and those offered by CARESEARCH will be expensive. Under the community care legislation that came into effect in April 1993, those wanting to go into residential accommodation have to apply to their social services department for help with fees (previously it was the Department of Social Security). People now have to pass a 'needs test' as well as a 'means test'. It is probably as well to apply to the social services department for an assessment, therefore, before finding out what may be available in case you find that the options are just not affordable.

Residential accommodation for disabled young people is provided by organisations such as MENCAP. The Learning Disability Helpline (0808 8081111) will be able to give you more information.

Sexuality and relationships
A disabled young person's developing sexuality is often an area of great concern to parents. Many parents find it hard to believe that their son or daughter - because they have a learning disability - has sexual needs and sometimes feel that the idea of sex has been put into their minds by staff at school or day centres.

It is important to remember, however, that once your disabled son or daughter has reached his or her teens, physical changes will occur as with any other young adult, and with it the need for sexual fulfilment and close intimate relationships. Schools and day centres will hold lessons on sex education and relationships. It is important that your son or daughter is able to attend and make use of these sessions: being ignorant of sex will not make the need go away so it is best that s/he learns as much as possible about sexuality, relationships and the importance of contraception and so on.

An organisation which has information on sex and disability is the Family Planning Association. They also run courses on sex education and personal relationships which are geared to the needs of disabled people. Find out what is on in your area by contacting the fpa (formerly the Family Planning Association (address at the end of this chapter).

86

Registering as a disabled person

There are two types of register for disabled people: the local authority register and the disabled person's register.

The Local Authority Register

Every local authority has to keep a register of disabled adults under the Chonically Sick and Disabled Persons Act. Registration is voluntary but there is nothing to lose by registering. In fact, registration will help you get access to some services, such as a travel permit and a telephone. Children can also register to obtain this type of help. Ask your local social services office for details about registering.

Under the Children Act 1989, local authorities also have to set up registers of disabled children. This is to aid planning for future services, and for this reason it is important that you register your child, although it is voluntary and will not mean that you get a better access to services.

The Disabled Person Register

This is a register kept by the Disability Employment Adviser at the Job Centre of disabled people who are able to work and wish to do so. Young people aged between 16 and 18 can join the register at the Careers Office. Registration is voluntary but may be beneficial for several reasons: a) every employer with 20 or more workers has a duty to employ a proportion of registered disabled people; b) sheltered employment is generally reserved for registered disabled people; c) registered disabled people can be helped to take up an ordinary job, including help with fares to and from work, special equipment, adaptations of premises or equipment, and a personal reader for people with visual impairment; d) vacancies for car park attendants and passenger lift attendants are reserved for registered disabled people.

Parents and letting go

When any young person reaches adolescence, a parent must start the emotional process of letting go of their child. Their son or daughter is no longer completely dependent on them, a parent's role needs to change and their relationship with their son or daughter needs to be reassessed and re-evaluated. For some parents, this time is met with a sense of relief; for others, it represents a strong sense of loss.

These issues present themselves when a disabled young person reaches his or her teenage years, but perhaps to a greater extent. Parents have to grapple with their young person's physical changes, their developing sexuality and independence, whilst at the same time still needing to take much of the initiative in regard to sorting out his or her future education, work and living options.

Most parents, understandably, feel anxious about their disabled son or daughter moving away from home. Some parents never consider this to be an option and continue caring for their son or daughter until they are too old or unwell to do so. Some parents who feel concerned about this sort of situation arising look at the options earlier on, before any crisis occurs, and then find it extremely hard to let go. If they are older parents, they have probably devoted much of their lives to caring for their disabled son or daughter and cannot see any role or life beyond this.

There are no easy answers to these very real dilemmas. The best parents can do is discuss what they feel and the options available for their son or daughter with a professional, such as a social worker or an adviser at their local voluntary organisation for the disabled. Counseling, information and support are the only things which can help parents in this situation so do not be afraid to be open and honest in requesting help.

Now read the key points overleaf.

KEY POINTS

- At age 16, disabled young people can claim benefits in their own right, regardless of their parents' income or savings. Benefits that can be claimed are Incapacity Benefit, Income Support, Disability Living Allowance and Working Tax Credit.

- All young people have a right to education up to the age of 19. Talk to your son or daughter's school and the Connexions Personal Advisor about the options, which may include staying on at school, attending a college or day centre or Youth Training.

- Work opportunities include ordinary employment and sheltered employment. Speak to a Connexions Personal Advisor about different work opportunities. Registering as a disabled person at the Job Centre may be helpful in gaining ordinary employment.

- Living options include independent living or residential care. Ask your social service department for an assessment.

- Sexuality and relationships are an important part of growing up for all young people, including those who are disabled. Organisations such as fpa (family planning association) provide information, advice and courses on sex and disability.

- The transition from childhood to adulthood and the possibility of a young person moving away from home can present parents with a complex host of emotions and dilemmas. Talking to someone about these feelings is important as is obtaining information and advice and the options open to your son or daughter. Talk to social services or your local voluntary organisation.

USEFUL ORGANISATIONS

Skill: National Bureau for Students with Disabilities
4th Floor, Chapter House, 18-20 Crucifix Lane, London SE1 3JW.
020 7450 0620
Information Service: 0800 328 5050
Email: info@skill.org.uk
www.skill.org.uk

RADAR (Royal Association for Disability and Rehabilitation)
12 City Forum, 250 City Road, London EC1V 8AF
020 7250 3222
www.radar.org.uk

MENCAP (Royal Society for Mentally Handicapped Children and Adults)
123 Golden Lane, London, EC1Y ORT
020 7454 0454
www.mencap.org.uk
Learning Disability Helpline: 0808 8081111

REMPLOY LTD
Stonecourt
Siskin Drive
Coventry CV3 4FJ
0800 138 7656
www.remploy.co.uk

COMMUNITY SERVICE VOLUNTEERS
237 Pentonville Road, London N1 9NJ
020 7278 6601
www.csv.org.uk

CROSSROAD CARING FOR CARERS
10 Regent Place, Rugby, Warwickshire CV21 2PN
01788 573653
www.crossroads.org.uk

LEONARD CHESHIRE FOUNDATION
30 Millbank, London SW1P 4QD
020 7802 8200
www.leonard-cheshire.org.uk

CARELINE
Cardinal Heenan Centre, 326 High Road, Ilford, Essex 1G1 1QP
020 8514 5444
Helpline: 0845 122 8622 (Mon-Fri 10-1 and 7-10 pm)

Confidential counseling service for children, young people and adults.

CARESEARCH
ARC House
Marsden House
Chesterfield
Derbyshire SO40 1JY
01246 555043
www.24dr.com/reference/contact/group/caresearch.htm

CARE CHOICES LTD
Valley Court, Croydon, Nr. Royston, Herts SG8 OHF
Helpline: 01223 207770
www.carechoices.co.uk/scr

Publishes 'The Care Homes Select Directory'.

Connexions
www.connexions.gov.uk

Advice line open 8am-2am

080 800 13219

HOUSING OPTIONS
Stanelaw House
Sutton Lane
Sutton
Witney
Oxfordshire OX29 5RY
0845 4561497
www.housingoptions.org.uk

Housing advisory service for people with learning disabilities.

RATHBONE
Head Office, 4th Floor, Church Gate House,
56 Oxford Street, Manchester, M1 6EU
0800 731 5321
www.rathboneuk.org

Information, advice and outreach services for independent living, vocational training and employment opportunities for young people with learning disabilities.

fpa (formerly Family Planning Association)
2-12 Pentonville Road, London N1 9FP
020 7837 5432
www.fpa.org.uk

8

THE LAW AND HOW TO MAKE A COMPLAINT

It is a fact that disabled children and their families have a right to services to improve the quality of their lives. This right is a legal one and is explicit in a number of pieces of legislation, which are outlined in this chapter. Knowing the legislation under which you are entitled to certain services can often help in gaining access to them so do not be afraid to quote the law. It is also important to know how to make a formal and official complaint if necessary. Being in a position of needing to ask for services and help can make you feel powerless: knowing your legal rights and how to complain will give you a little more control over obtaining the help you need. The law is very complex and the descriptions of the relevant legislation given below are very brief and basic. If you need more details or specialist legal advice it is advisable to see someone at your local Citizens Advice Bureau or a Solicitor if you have one.

The Children Act 1989
The Children Act 1989, which came into force in October 1991, is the first piece of legislation for children which includes disabled children and at last recognises that children with disabilities are children first.

The Children Act introduces the concept of a child "in need". Children in need include:
(i) children whose health and welfare may suffer significantly without services from the local authority;
(ii) disabled children.

Under the Children Act 1989, a disabled child is a child who is: "blind, deaf or dumb or suffers from mental disorder of any kind or is substantially and permanently handicapped by illness, injury or congenital deformity or such other disability as may be prescribed;" The local authority which provides services for children includes social services, housing, education and leisure services. Other services which may be offered are provided by the health authority and/or local voluntary organisations. The local authority must do the following for children in need, including disabled children:

- provide day care for under 5s;
- provide after school and holiday supervised activities;
- set up a register of children with disabilities;
- publish information about services;
- provide services designed to give children with disabilities the opportunity to lead lives which are as normal as possible.

Examples of services depend on what the local authority views as appropriate but may include home helps, family centres, respite care, financial assistance for holidays etc.,

- provide services which take account of a child's race, religion, culture and language;
- set up a complaints procedure;
- provide services which protect and promote the welfare of all children, including the duty to investigate all allegations of abuse and/or neglect;
- provide a high standard of care for children who are being looked after by the local authority, in foster or residential homes;
- seek the views of children and parents/carers, when working with families and planning services, and work at all times in partnership with families.

95

The Children Act 2004 and other recent government policy

The *Children Act 2004* is the legal underpinning for government policy towards children outlined in the government Green Paper, *Every Child Matters*, 2003. This document outlined 5 main outcomes the government want to see for all children in the UK. These are that children should: be healthy, stay safe, enjoy and achieve, make a positive contribution and achieve economic wellbeing. In order to achieve some of these outcomes for children, the Children Act 2004 aims to transform services for children by ensuring that health, social care and education services for children work closely together and offer an integrated and 'joined up' approach. These integrated services will be provided in children's centres, children's trusts and children's services. For disabled children, this should mean that services and professionals for you and your child work more closely together, perhaps in the same multi-disciplinary team and/or in the same office.

The Children Act 2004 does not change your entitlements under the Children Act 1989 as the more recent piece of legislation is more about how services should be delivered.

Other important policy produced by the government aiming to include aims to improve the quality of life for disabled children and young people, include the report *Improving the Life Chances of Disabled People* (2004) and *Valuing People* (2001).

The Education Act 1996, The Special Educational Needs and Disability Act 2001 and special educational needs

The Education Act 1996 specifies the powers and duties of Local Authority Education Departments in providing for the special educational needs (SEN) of children with disabilities.

The main duties of LEAs under the Education Act 1996 is to identify special educational needs of children for whom they are responsible and to make the special educational provision which they need.

Schools and local education authorities are required to have regard to the Code of Practice on the identification and assessment of special educational needs. The Code recommends that schools should identify children's needs and take action to meet those needs as early as possible, working with parents. The Code says that schools should deal with children's needs in stages.

The Special Educational Needs and Disability Act 2001, which came into force in January 2002, has changed Part 4 of the Education Act 1996, which covered special educational needs and has introduced new anti-discrimination duties on education providers. The stages of the Code of Practice , which accompanies this legislation are outlined in chapter 4.

The Special Educational Needs and Disability Act 2001 has introduced new statutory duties on local education authorities and schools, which includes a stronger right for children with special educational needs to be educated at a mainstream school, a new right for schools to request a statutory assessment of a child and new duties on local educational authorities to arrange for parents of children with special educational needs to be provided with services offering advice and information and a means of resolving disputes.

The Chronically Sick and Disabled Persons Act 1970
Under this piece of legislation, the local authority has a duty to establish numbers of disabled people in their area, to determine their needs and publicise services. It is also the duty of the local authority to arrange any of the following services (where satisfied it is necessary):

- practical assistance in the home;

- help with radio and TV;

- library and recreational facilities;

- help to take up facilities outside the home;

- assistance with travel (permits and orange badge scheme);

- help with holidays, telephones, aids and adaptations.

Finally, the local authority has a duty to provide access for disabled people in certain buildings to which the public have access.

NHS and Community Care Act 1990

The Act emphasises a care management approach and assessment based on individual need. It requires a close partnership between professionals and service users in assessing and designing tailor-made packages of care. This piece of legislation emphasises the importance of dividing the purchasing of care from the provision of care, and puts great emphasis on the independent sector to provide social care.

The Act also says that Community Care plans must be published and reviewed by each local authority, in consultation with health authorities, housing and voluntary agencies representing service users and carers.

A needs assessment must be carried out where it appears to the local authority that any person for whom they may provide or arrange community care services, may be in need of such services. Where services of the health or housing authorities may be needed, the local authority should notify them and invite their assistance.

Where a needs assessment has been carried out , the local authority shall then decide whether services should be provided. Care may be provided before a needs assessment, where urgently necessary, with an assessment carried out as soon as possible afterwards.

Carers and Recognition of Services Act 1995

This Act requires local authorities to assess the needs of carers of disabled people, including disabled children, and people who are chronically sick, including young carers.

Carers and Disabled Children Act 2000

This Act was implemented in April 2001. It reinforces the rights of carers under the 1995 Carers Act and states that parent carers are entitled to an assessment in their own right. It also outlines the rights and services that can be provided to families of disabled children under the Children Act 1989.

Under this legislation, young disabled people aged 16 and 17 years can receive direct payments for services they have been assessed by social services to need, so they can arrange and pay for services themselves (see Community Care (Direct Payments) Act 1996 below).

Employment Act 2002

Gives parents of disabled children under 18 the right to request flexible working hours.

The Carers (Equal Opportunities) Act 2004

This piece of legislation places a duty on social services to inform carers of their rights to an assessment and to ensure that health and social care services work more closely together in supporting carers.

The Childcare Act 2006

Under this legislation, local authorities have a duty to provide childcare for parents with disabled children up to the age of 18 and to improve the provision of information about services for disabled children.

Community Care (Direct Payments Act 1996)

If a disabled person is between the ages of 16 (previously 18) and 65, s/he can ask the social services department for direct payments for services; ie. money to pay for care services themselves. Ask your local social services department for more information.

Housing Grants Construction and Regeneration Act 1996 (England and Wales).

Disabled Facilities Grant

Under Part 1 of the Housing Grants, Construction and Regeneration Act 1996 local housing authorities are able to give Disabled Facilities Grants to disabled people, including disabled children, to help with the cost of adaptations to enable them to live as independently as possible in their own homes.

The main underlying principle is that disabled people should be able to enjoy comparable facilities in their homes to those enjoyed by able-bodied people. The grant is therefore designed to address the adaptation needs to which a person's ability gives rise by providing:

- mandatory grant for adaptation works of an essential nature up to £25,000 in England

- discretionary grant for a wide range of works which go beyond basic housing requirements

The purposes for which the Mandatory Disabled Facilities Grant can be given are:

- facilitating access to and from the dwelling

- facilitating access to living rooms, bedrooms and bathroom in the dwelling and facilitating use of facilities in bathroom

- facilitating preparation and cooking of food by a disabled person

- improving the heating system in the dwelling and facilitating use by a disabled person of control over sources of power, heat or light

- making the dwelling safe for the disabled occupant and others residing with him or her

A discretionary Disabled Facilities Grant can be given to make a dwelling suitable for the accommodation, welfare or employment of a disabled person or to "top up" the grant for a mandatory adaptation costing more than £25,000 in England

A local authority is only able to approve a Disabled Facilities Grant where it is satisfied that the works are suitable to meet the disabled persons needs. The amount of grant awarded is subject to a means test. For disabled children or young people up to their 18th birthday the "test of resources" is applied to the joint income of both parents if they live together, or to the child's main carer. 18 year olds and young people of 16 or 17 claiming benefits in their own right will be assessed on their own income. Housing authorities must ensure the works for which the grant are sought are "necessary and appropriate" to meet the needs of a disabled person/child. The local authority must also decide if it is "reasonable and practicable" to carry them out in a particular dwelling. If it is impracticable other options (such as re-housing) may need to be explored.

Disability Discrimination Act 1995

If you think you have been discriminated against you can take legal action against the organization. The legisation covers employment (eg. organizations with over 15 employees have to make 'reasonable adjustments' to the workplace to accommodate a disabled person) and goods, services and facilities (eg. Refusing to serve disabled people is illegal unless 'justified'. Aids should be provided where 'reasonable'). From 2004, properties, educational establishments and transport must be made more accessible to disabled people.

Disability Discrimination Act 2005

This extends the provision made under the DDA 1995 to make sure that public bodies are promoting equality of opportunity for all disabled people.

HOW TO MAKE A COMPLAINT

Health

If you have a problem with your G.P., it is best to discuss this with the surgery first. If you want to take the matter further, you should contact the Family Health Services Authority (FHSA), Health Board in Scotland or Health and Social Services Board in Northern Ireland. The address will be in your local telephone directory. You could also contact your local Community Health Council (CHC), Local Health Council in Scotland or District Committee for Health and Social Services in Northern Ireland.

If you have a complaint about treatment you or your child has received in hospital, you should try and deal with it in stages: first, it is best to discuss the complaint informally with a member of staff; second, if your complaint cannot be dealt with informally you could take it to a complaints officer in the hospital, if they have one; third, if there is not a complaints officer or you are still not satisfied, you could write to the Chief Executive of the local Health Trust. You should also ask your local Community Health Council advice on doing this. Another avenue is the NHS Ombudsman, who investigates complaints to do with maladministration. Remember also that there is now a Health Service Patients' charter, which you can use when making a complaint.

Education

When dealing with your Local Education Authority (LEA), if at any stage you are unhappy with a decision, you should talk to your child's school or to the Named Officer who has dealt with your child's case. However, if you cannot come to an agreement with the LEA and/or you wish to make a complaint, you have a right to take the matter to the Special Educational Needs Tribunal.

You can appeal to the Special Educational Needs Tribunal if:

- the LEA refuse to make a statutory assessment of your child, after you have asked them to;

- the LEA refuse to make a statement for your child after an assessment;

- you disagree with parts 2,3 or 4 of your child's statement;

- your child already has a statement and the LEA refuse to assess your child again or change the name of the school in that statement;

- the LEA decide to stop maintaining your child's statement.

More information about the Special Educational Needs Tribunal can be obtained from your local LEA, in the form of a booklet.

Social Services

Since April 1991 all Social Services Departments have had to set up a formal complaints procedure. Your complaint will be investigated by an officer of the council and an independent person, who will both talk to you and any other relevant parties about your situation. The result of the investigation should be given to you in writing, after which you may take the matter further to the Independent Review Panel if you are still not satisfied. Ask your local Social Services Department for details on how to use the procedure.

Housing

If you want to make a complaint about a housing matter which is related to a disability, such as a delay in doing adaptations to your home, for example, RADAR may be able to help you make a complaint. You could also contact the Local Government Ombudsman if there has been any maladministration.

Further help with making a complaint

When making a complaint about health, education, social services, housing or any other issue, you could try and contact your local councillor or M.P. You will be able to find our how to do this by contacting your local council or by asking at your local Citizens Advice Bureau, who may also be able to help with your complaint.

KEY POINTS

- Knowing your legal rights and how to make a complaint can help give you more control over the services you and your disabled child receive.

- You and your child have a right to services under the Children Act 1989, the Education Act 1996, Special Needs and Disability Act 2001, the Chronically Sick and Disabled Persons Act 1970, the NHS and Community Care Act 1990, the Carers Act 1995, Carers and Disabled Children Act 2000, the Disability Discrimination Act 1995, Community Care (Direct Payments) Act 1996 and the Housing Grants and Reconstruction Act (1996).

- Making a complaint is sometimes necessary and can often help improve services for other disabled children and their families. Most council departments and the health service have their own procedures but there are outside bodies you can use, such as the Community Health Council, the Special Educational Needs Tribunal and your local councillor or M.P. The Citizens Advice Bureau may also be able to advise you.

USEFUL ORGANISATIONS

Children's Legal Centre
University of Essex
Wivenhoe Park
Colchester CO4 3SQ
01206 872466 (advice line Mon-Fri 10-12.30 & 2-4.30 pm)
Education Law Advice Line 0845 456681
Email ck@essex.ac.uk
www.childrenslegalcentre.com

Disability Law Service
39-45 Cavell Street
London E1 2BP
020 7791 9800 (Mon-Fri 10.30-1 & 2-5 pm)

Advisory Centre for Education (ACE)
1b Aberdeen Studios
22 Highbury Grove
London N5 2EA
0808 800 5793 (freephone advice line Mon-Fri 2-5pm)
www.ae-ed.org.uk

RADAR (Royal Association for Disability and Rehabilitation)
12 City Forum
250 City Road
London EC1V 8AF
020 7250 0212
radar@radar.org.uk
www.radar.org.uk

Disability Alliance
Universal House

88-94 Wentworth Street
London E1 7SA
020 7247 8765
www.disabilityalliance.org

Disability Rights Commission
DRC Helpline
Freepost
MID 02164
Stratford upon Avon CV37 9BR
0845 7622 633
Office.da@dial.pipex.com
www.disability.gov.com

Local Authority Ombudsmen
Commission for Local Administration in England
21 Queen Anne's Gate
London SW1H 9BU
020 7915 3210

The Oaks
Westwood Way
Westwood Business Park
Coventry CV4 8JB
024 76695999

Beverley House
17 Shipton Road
York YO30 5FZ
01904 663 200

Commission for Local Administration in Wales
Derwen House
Court Road
Bridgend
Wales CF31 1BN
01656 661325

Commissioner for Local Administration in Scotland
23 Walker Street
Edinburgh EH3 7HX
0131 225 5300

Commissioner for Complaints
Progressive House
33 Willington Place
Belfast BT1 6HN
028 90 233 821

Useful Reading

Factsheets produced by Contact a Family (www.cafamily.org.uk)

When your child has additional needs

Living without a diagnosis

Working and caring for a disabled child

Dealing with debt

Tax credits-overpayments

Family checklist

A genetic condition in the family

Holidays, play and leisure

Transition

A guide to assessments and services

Special educational needs

Aids, equipment and adaptations

Relationships and caring for a disabled child

Finding and paying for childcare

Benefits, tax credits and other financial assistance

The tax credits guide.

Information from Radar (www.radar.org.uk)

Holidays in Britain and Ireland 2007-02-28

Children First-services for disabled children 2006

Publications from Disability Alliance (www.disabilityalliance.org)

Disability Rights Handbook

Don't Miss Out-A Guide to benefits and services for disabled children and their families

Tell it like it is! A guide to claiming Disability Living Allowance for a child with disabilities or special needs.

Motability (www.motability.co.uk)

A Guide to the Motability scheme

From the Department of Education and Skills

Special Educational needs (SEN) A Guide for parents

For young people aged 16+

Useful information from www.after16.org.uk

General books

All Together (2003) by Mary Dickins and Judy Denziloe. National Children's Bureau.

Growing Up With a Disability (1998) Carol Robinson and Kirsten Stalker. Jessica Kingsley.

Disabled Children and the Law: Research and Good Practice (2006) by Janet Read, Luke Clements and David Ruebain. Jessica Kingsley.

Different Dads: Father's stories of parenting Disabled Children (2007) by David Cameron, Jill Harrison, Matthew Henderson and Rob Leonard. Jessica Kingsley.

Brothers and Sisters of Disabled Children (2003) by Peter Burke. Jessica Kingsley.

Useful Organisations

Each chapter has a list of useful organisations relevant to that particular topic or topics. This list comprises the main national organisations you may find useful, some of which have already been mentioned in other chapters.

Action for Sick Children (NAWCH)
36 Jacksons Edge Road
Disley
Stockport
SK12 2JL
0800 0744519
www.actionforsickchildren.org

ADD/ADHD Family Support Group
Helpline 01454 772262

AFASIC – Overcoming Speech Impairments
2nd Floor, 50-52 Great Sutton Street, London EC1V ODJ
020 7490 9410
Helpline: 08453 555577
www.afasic.org.uk

Association for Brain Damaged Children
Clifton House, 3 St Paul's Road, Foleshill, Coventry CV6 5DE
02476 665450

Association for Spina Bifida and Hydrocephalus (ASBAH)
42 Park Road, Peterborough, PE1 2UQ
Helpline 0845 4507755 Mon-Fri 10-4

British Dyslexia Association
98 London Road, Reading, RG1 5AU

Helpline: 0118 966 8271/2677
www.bdadyslexia.org.uk

Brittle Bone Society
30 Guthrie Street, Dundee DD1 5BS
01382 204 446
www.brittlebone.org
Helpline 08000 28 2459

Carers' National Association
Ruth Pitter House, 20-25 Glasshouse Yard, London EC1A 4JN
020 7490 8818
Carers' Line: 0808 808 7777
www.carersuk..org.uk

Contact a Family
209-211 City Road, London EC1V 1JN
020 7608 8700
Helpline: 0808 808 3555 (Mon-Fri 10-4)
www.cafamily.org.uk

The Council for Disabled Children
8 Wakley Street, London EC1V 7QE
020 7843 6000
www.ncb.org.uk

Cystic Fibrosis Trust
11 London Road, Bromley, Kent BR1 1BY
020 8464 7211
Support: 0845 859 1000
Benefits: 0845 859 1010
Welfare: 0845 859 1020
www.cftrust.org.uk

DfES Publications Centre,
PO Box 5050, Sherwood Park, Annersley, Nottingham, NG15 ODJ.
0845 602 2260
Email: dfes@prolog.uk.com
www.dfes.gov.uk/sen

Disability Alliance
Universal House, 88-94 Wentworth Street, London E1 7SA
020 7247 8776
www.disabilityalliance.org

Down's Syndrome Association
Langdon Down Centre
2A Langdon park
Teddington
TW11 9PS
Helpline 0845 230 0372
www.dsa-uk.com

Dyspraxia Foundation
8 West Alley, Hitchin SG5 1EG
01462 454986
www.dyspraxiafoundation.org.uk

Family Fund
Unit 4, Alpha Court
Monks Cross Drive
Huntington
York Y32 9WN
0845 130 4542
www.familyfund.org.uk

Epilepsy Association
New Anstey House, Gate Way Drive, Yeadon, Leeds LS19 7XY
0113 210 8800
Helpline 0808 800 5050
www.epilepsy.org.uk

Freidreich's Ataxia Group
Winchester House, Cranmer Road, London SW9
020 7582 1444
Helpline: 020 7820 3900

Haemophilia Society
First Floor Petersham House
57A Hatton Garden
London EC1 8JG
020 7831 1020
Freephone Helpline 0800 018 6068

Hyperactive Children's Support Group
71 Whyke Lane, Chichester, West Sussex PO19 2LD
01903 725182
www.hacsg.org.uk

MENCAP (Royal Society for Mentally Handicapped Children and Adults)
123 Golden Lane, London EC1Y ORT
020 7454 0454
www.mencap.org.uk

Learning Disability Helpline: 0808 8081111

Muscular Dystrophy Group of GB
Prescott House, 7-11 Prescott Place, London SW4 2BS

020 7720 8055
www.muscular-dystrophy.org

National Asthma Campaign
Providence House, Providence Place, London N1 ONT
020 7226 2260
Helpline: 08457 010203
www.asthma.org.uk

National Autistic Society
393 City Road, London EC1V 1NG
020 7833 2299
www.nas.org.uk

National Deaf Children's Society
15 Dufferin Street, London, EC1Y 8PD
020 7250 0123
www.ndcf.org.uk

National Eczema Society
Hill House, Highgate Hill, London N19 5NA
08702 413604

National Society for Epilepsy
Chesham Lane, Chalfont St Peter, Gerrards Cross, Bucks SL9 ORG
01494 601300
Helpline: 01494 601 400
www.epilepsynfe.org.uk

Royal National Institute for the Blind (RNIB)
105 Judd Street, London WC1H 9NE
020 7388 1266

Helpline: 0845 76 9999
Typetalk: 0800 51 51 52
www.rnib.org.uk

Royal National Institute for Deaf People (RNID)
19-23 Featherstone Street, London EC1Y 8SL
020 7296 8000
www.rnid.org.uk

SCOPE
6 Market Place, London N7 9PW
020 7619 7100
Helpline: 0800 626 216 (9am-9pm weekdays and 2-6 pm weekends)
www.scope.org.uk

SENSE (National Deaf-Blind and Rubella Association)
Laurel Leaf House, 11-13 Clifton Terrace, London N4 3SR
0845 1270060
www.sense.org.uk

Sickle Cell Society
54 Station Road, London NW10 4UA
020 8961 7795
www.sicklecellsociety.org

Tuberous Sclerosis Association of GB
PO Box 9644, Bromsgrove, B61 OFP
01527 871898
www.tuberous-sclerosis.org

Values Into Action
Oxford House, Derbyshire Street, London E2 6HG.
020 7729 5436

INDEX

www.straightforwardco.co.uk

All titles, listed below, in the Straightforward Guides Series can be purchased online, using credit card or other forms of payment by going to www.straightfowardco.co.uk A discount of 25% per title is offered with online purchases.

Law

A Straightforward Guide to:
Consumer Rights
Bankruptcy Insolvency and the Law
Employment Law
Private Tenants Rights
Family law
Small Claims in the County Court
Contract law
Intellectual Property and the law
Divorce and the law
Leaseholders Rights
The Process of Conveyancing
Knowing Your Rights and Using the Courts
Producing Your own Will
Housing Rights
The Bailiff the law and You
Probate and The Law
Company law
What to Expect When You Go to Court
Guide to Competition Law
Give me Your Money-Guide to Effective Debt Collection
Caring for a Disabled Child

General titles

Letting Property for Profit
Buying, Selling and Renting property
Buying a Home in England and France
Bookkeeping and Accounts for Small Business

Creative Writing
Freelance Writing
Writing Your own Life Story
Writing performance Poetry
Writing Romantic Fiction
Speech Writing

Teaching Your Child to Read and write
Teaching Your Child to Swim
Raising a Child-The Early Years

Creating a Successful Commercial Website
The Straightforward Business Plan
The Straightforward C.V.
Successful Public Speaking

Handling Bereavement
Play the Game-A Compendium of Rules
Individual and Personal Finance
Understanding Mental Illness
The Two Minute Message
Guide to Self Defence
Buying a Used Car
Tiling for Beginners

Go to:
www.straightforwardco.co.uk

Letting Property for Profit
Buying, Selling and Renting property
Buying a Home in England and France
Bookkeeping and Accounts for Small Business

Creative Writing
Freelance Writing
Writing Your own Life Story
Writing performance Poetry
Writing Romantic Fiction
Speech Writing

Teaching Your Child to Read and write
Teaching Your Child to Swim
Raising a Child-The Early Years

Creating a Successful Commercial Website
The Straightforward Business Plan
The Straightforward C.V.
Successful Public Speaking

Handling Bereavement
Play the Game-A Compendium of Rules
Individual and Personal Finance
Understanding Mental Illness
The Two Minute Message
Guide to Self Defence
Buying a Used Car